NURTURED FUTILITY
VOL III

SHEEP IN
WOLVES' CLOTHING

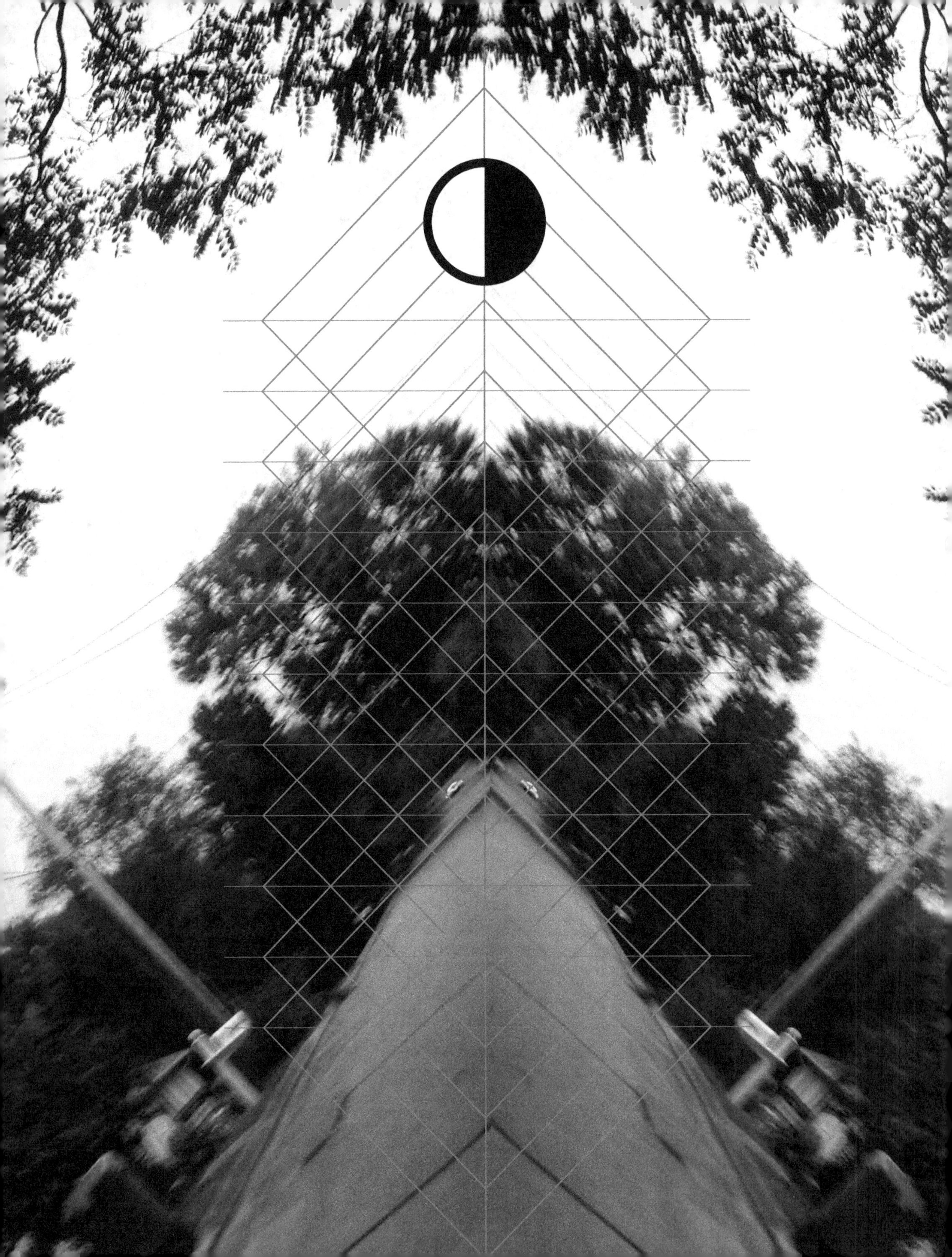

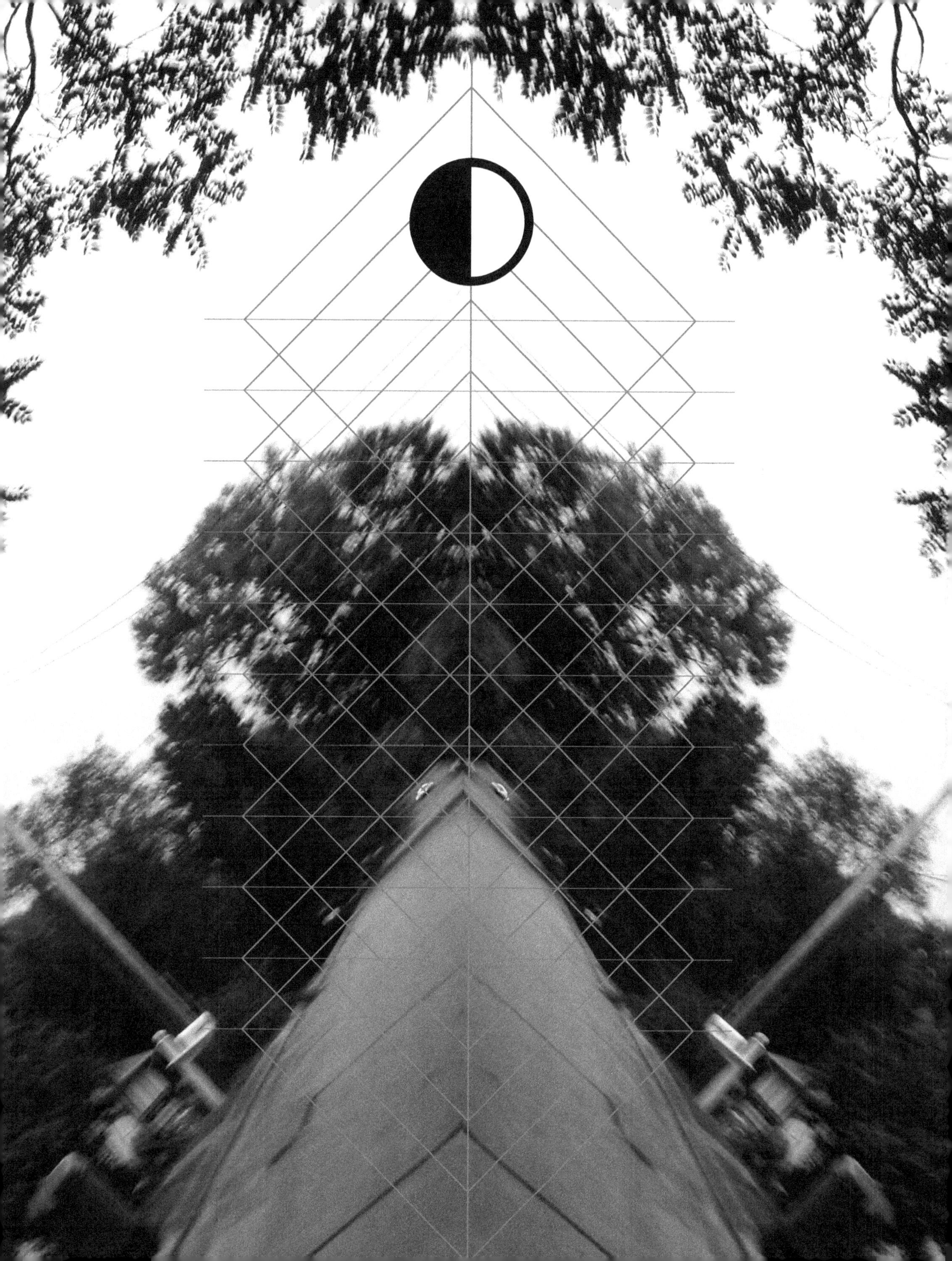

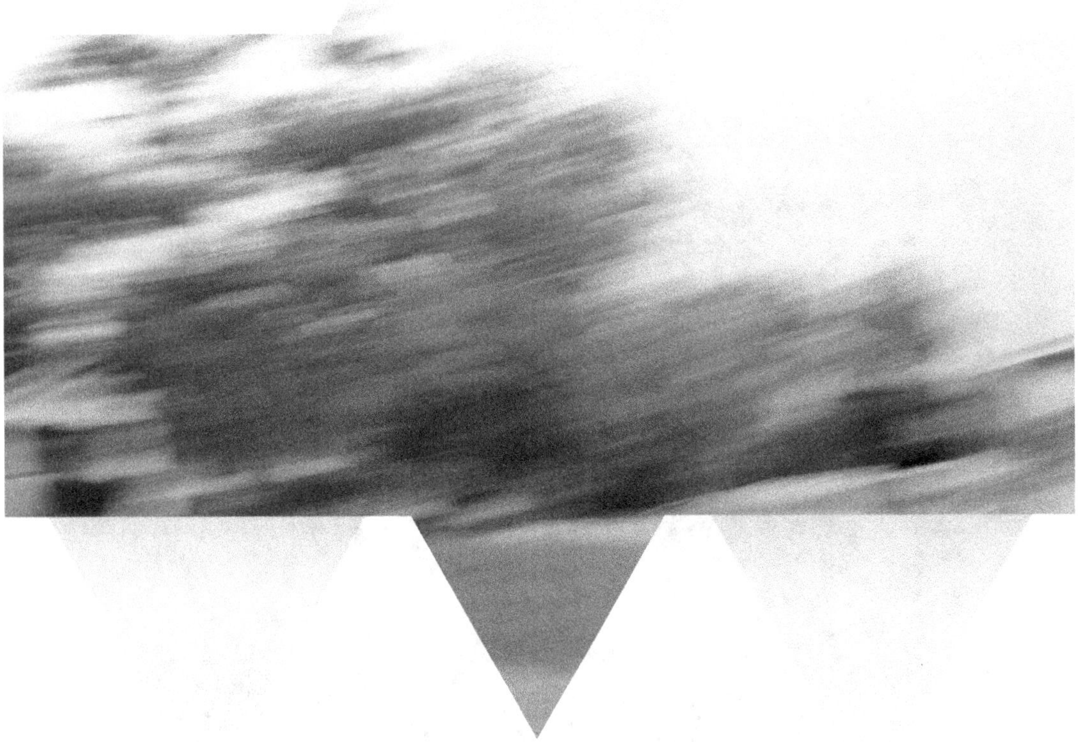

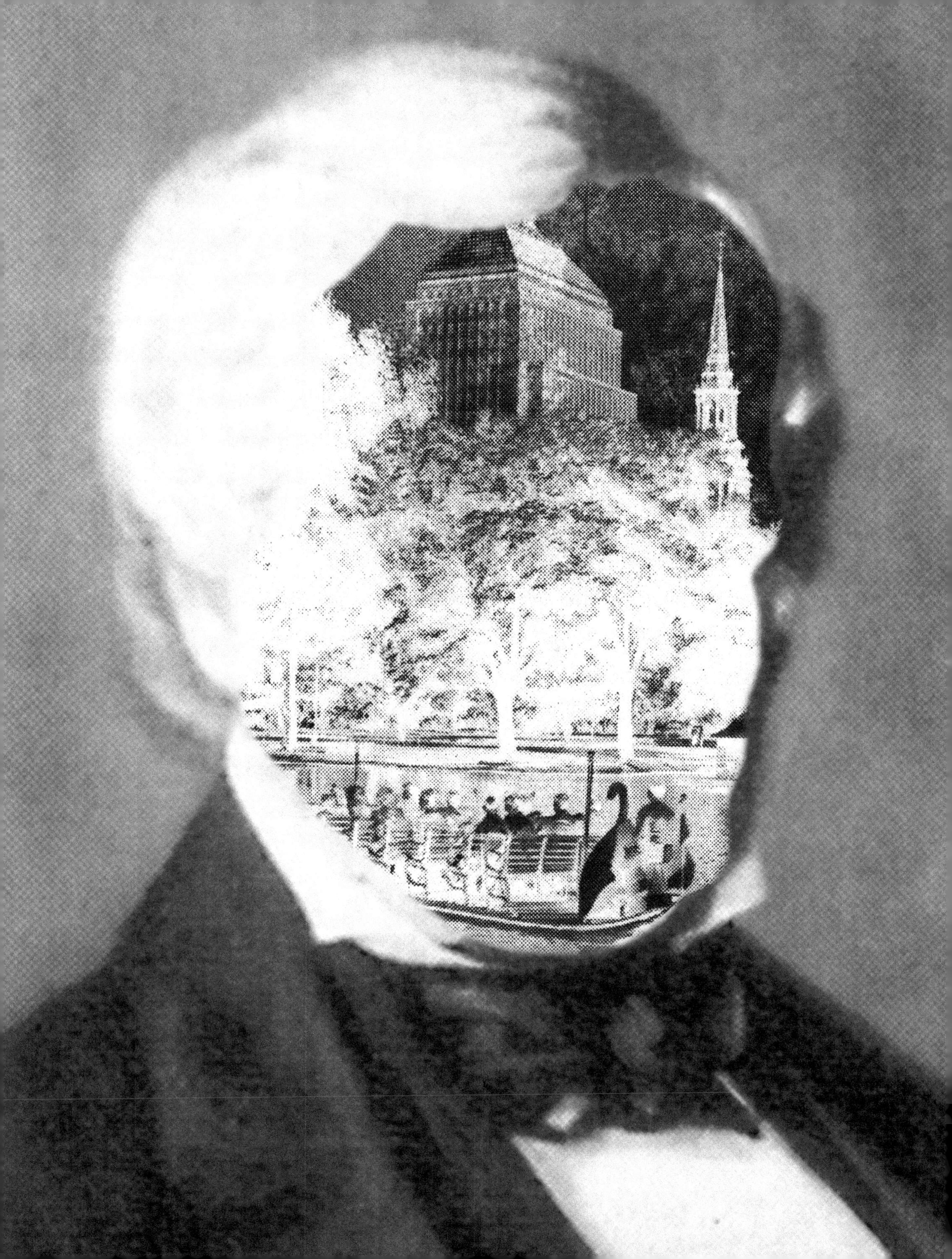

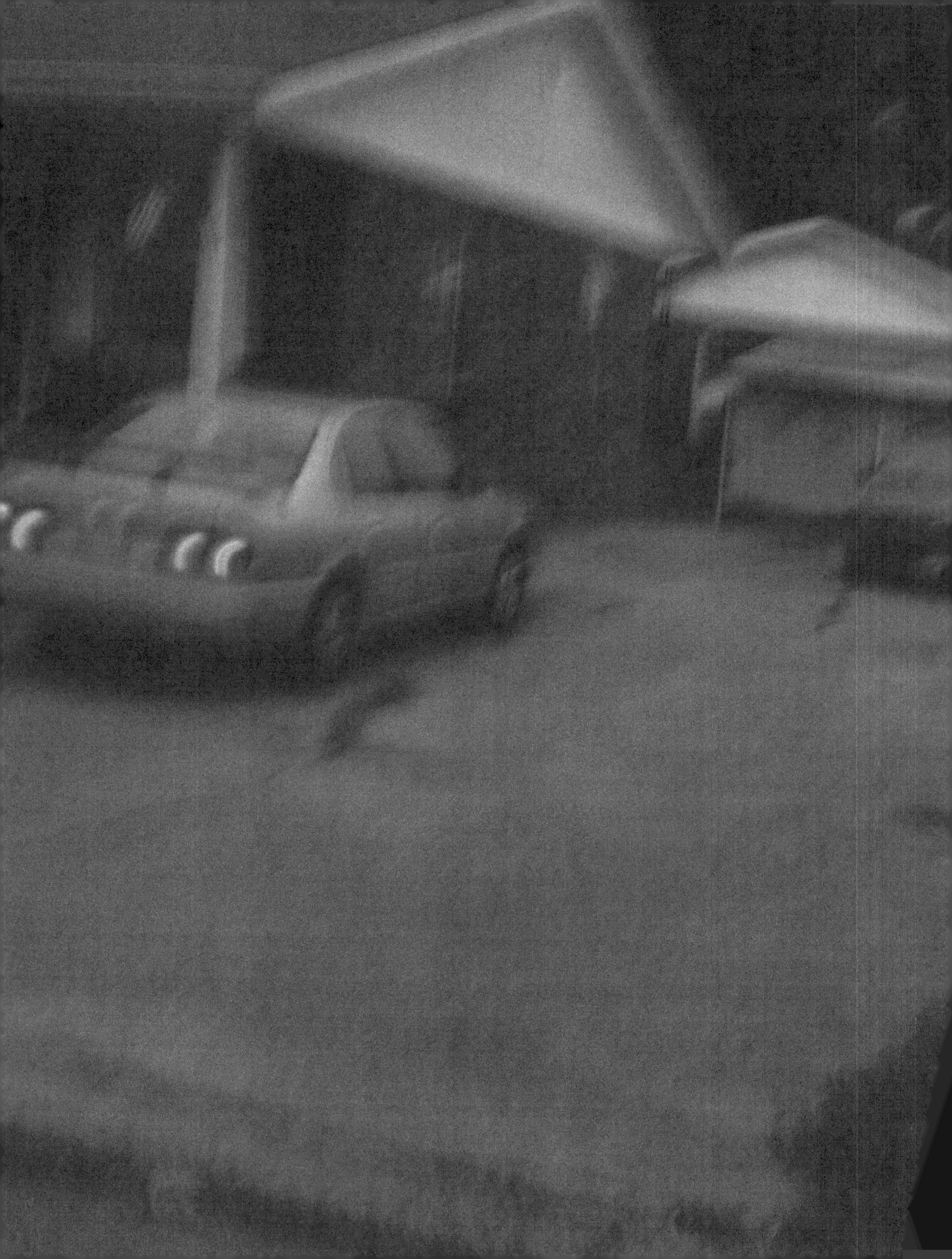

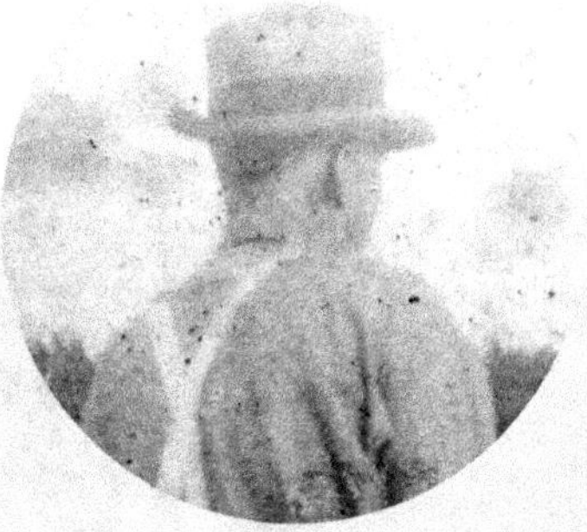

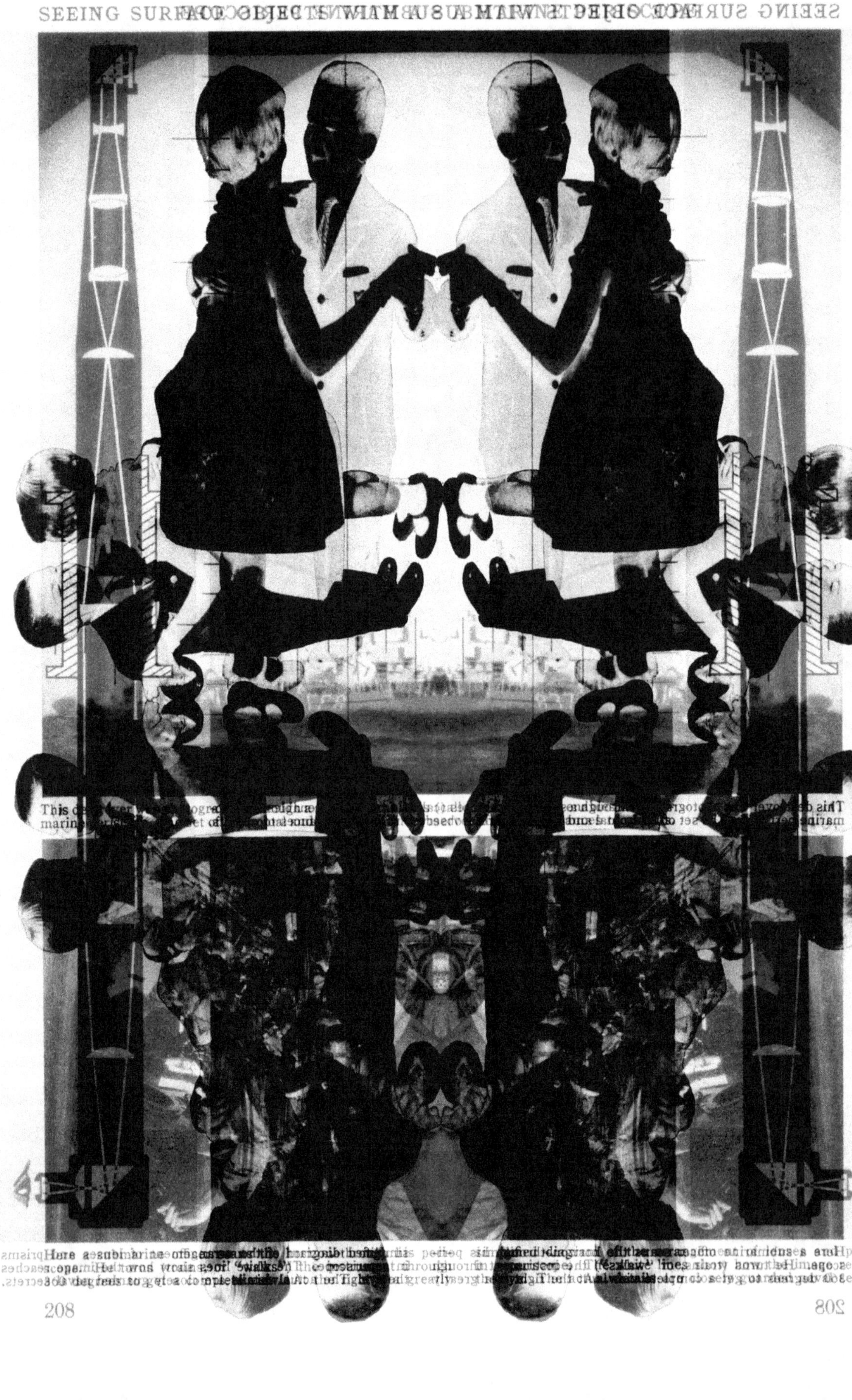
SEEING SURF
208

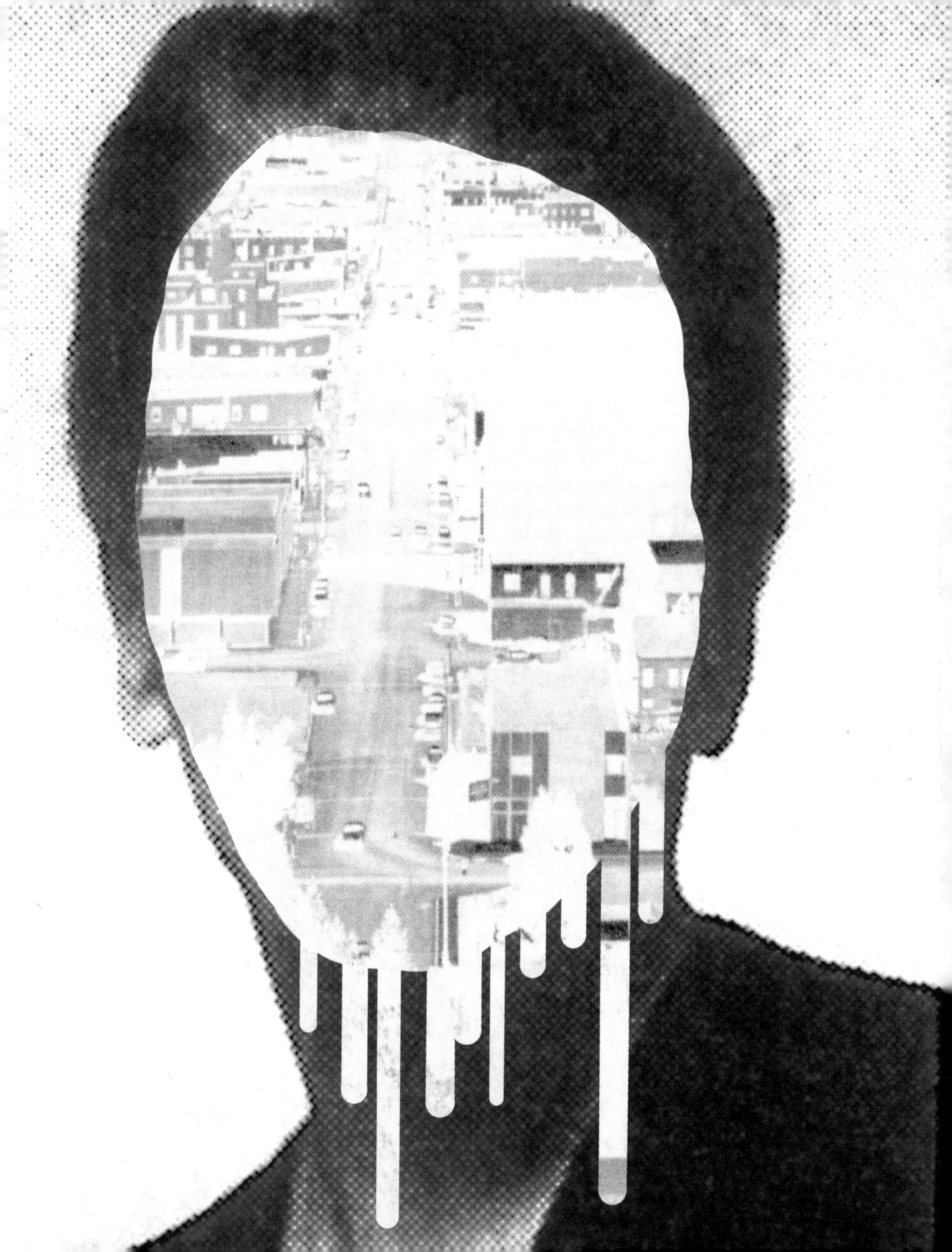

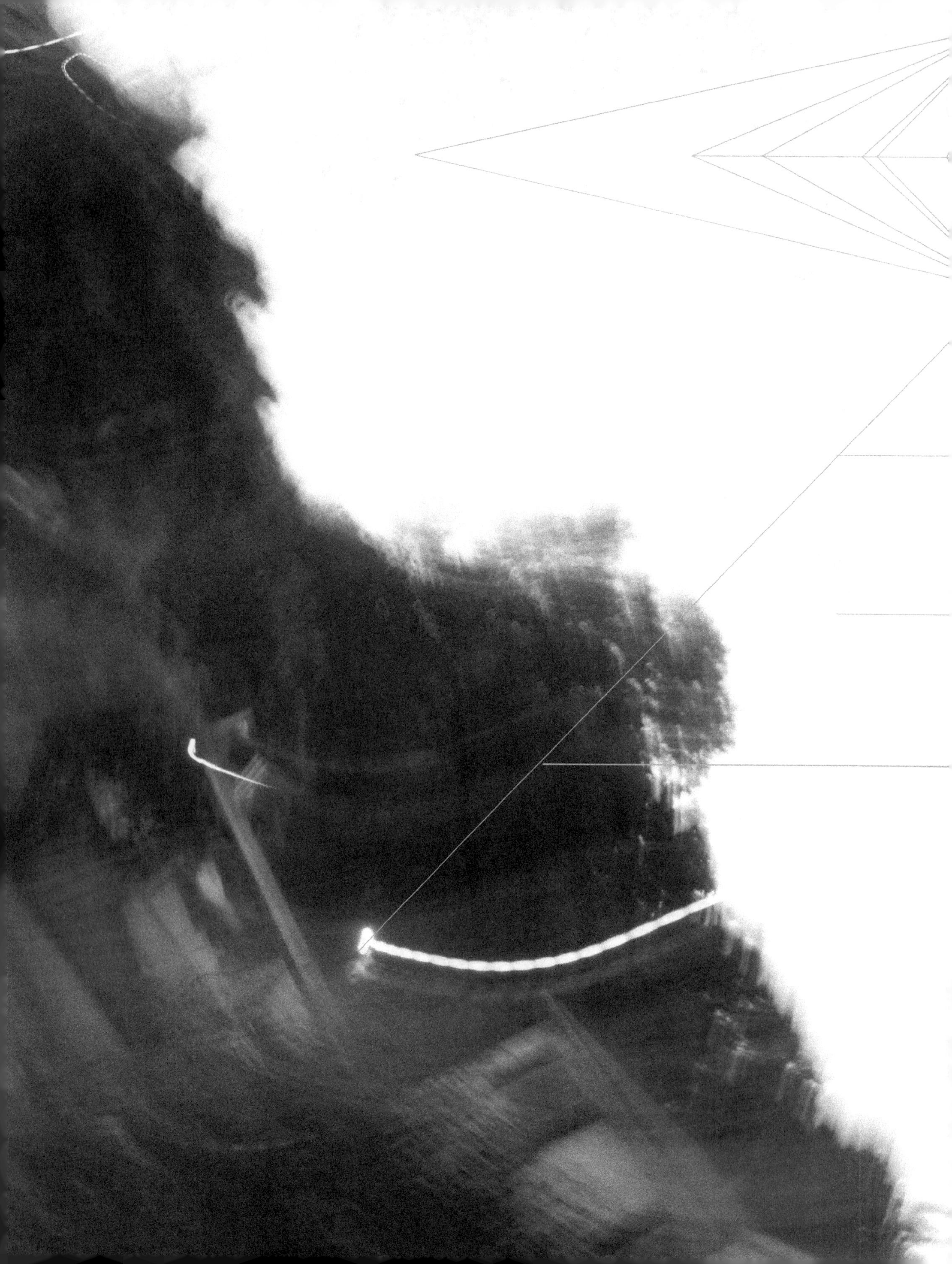

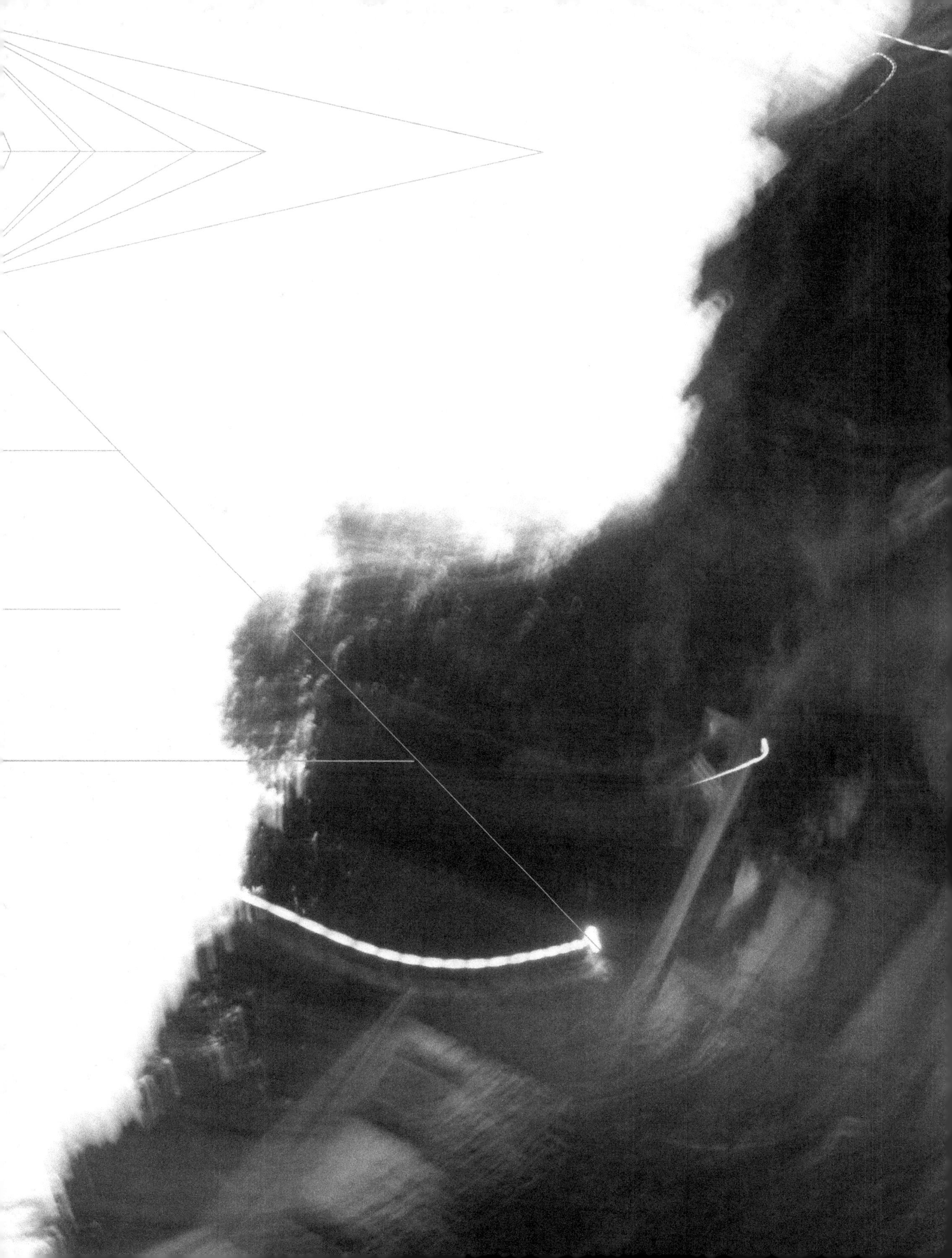

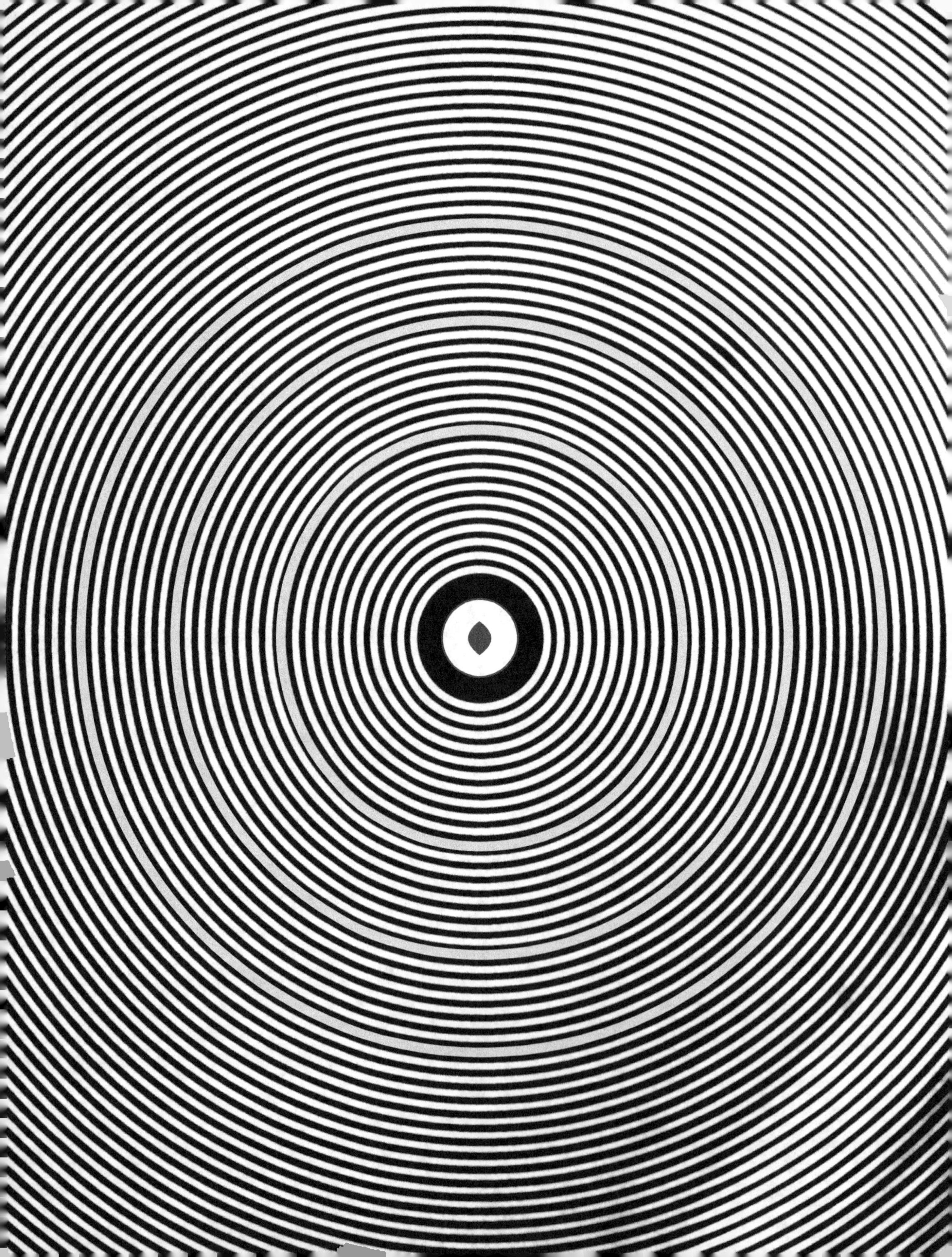

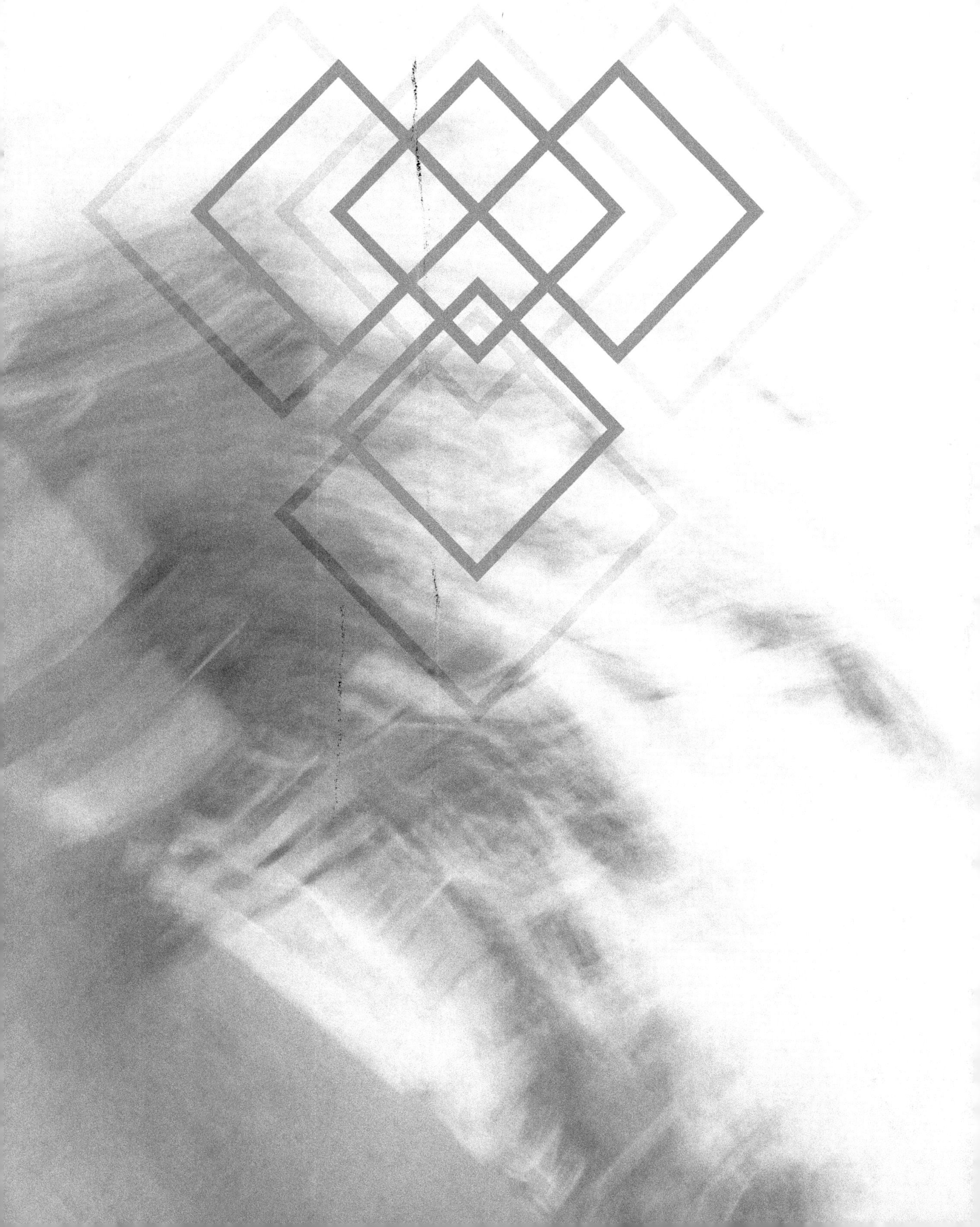

BIRTH OF A BLACK SWALLOWTAIL BUTTERFLY

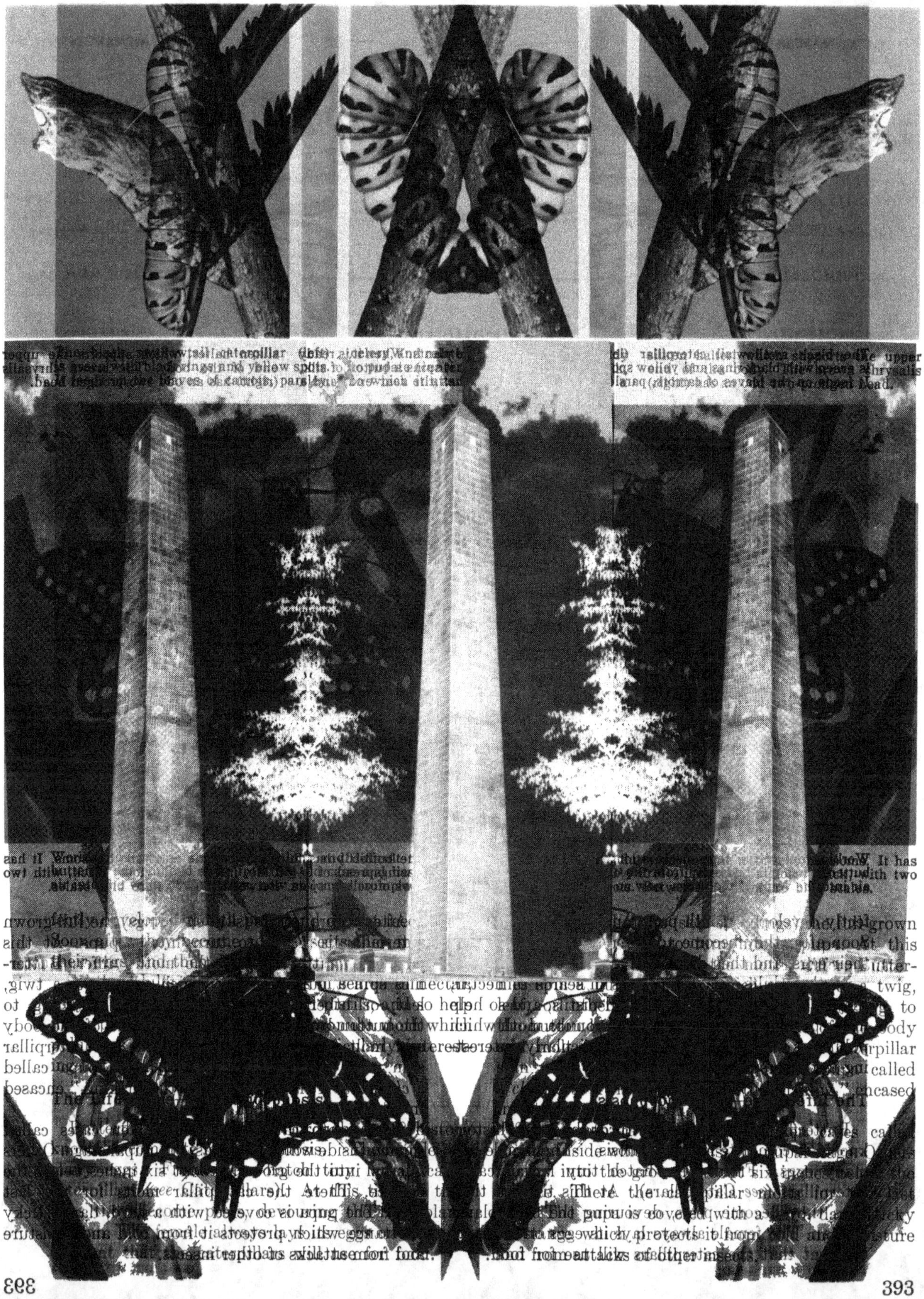

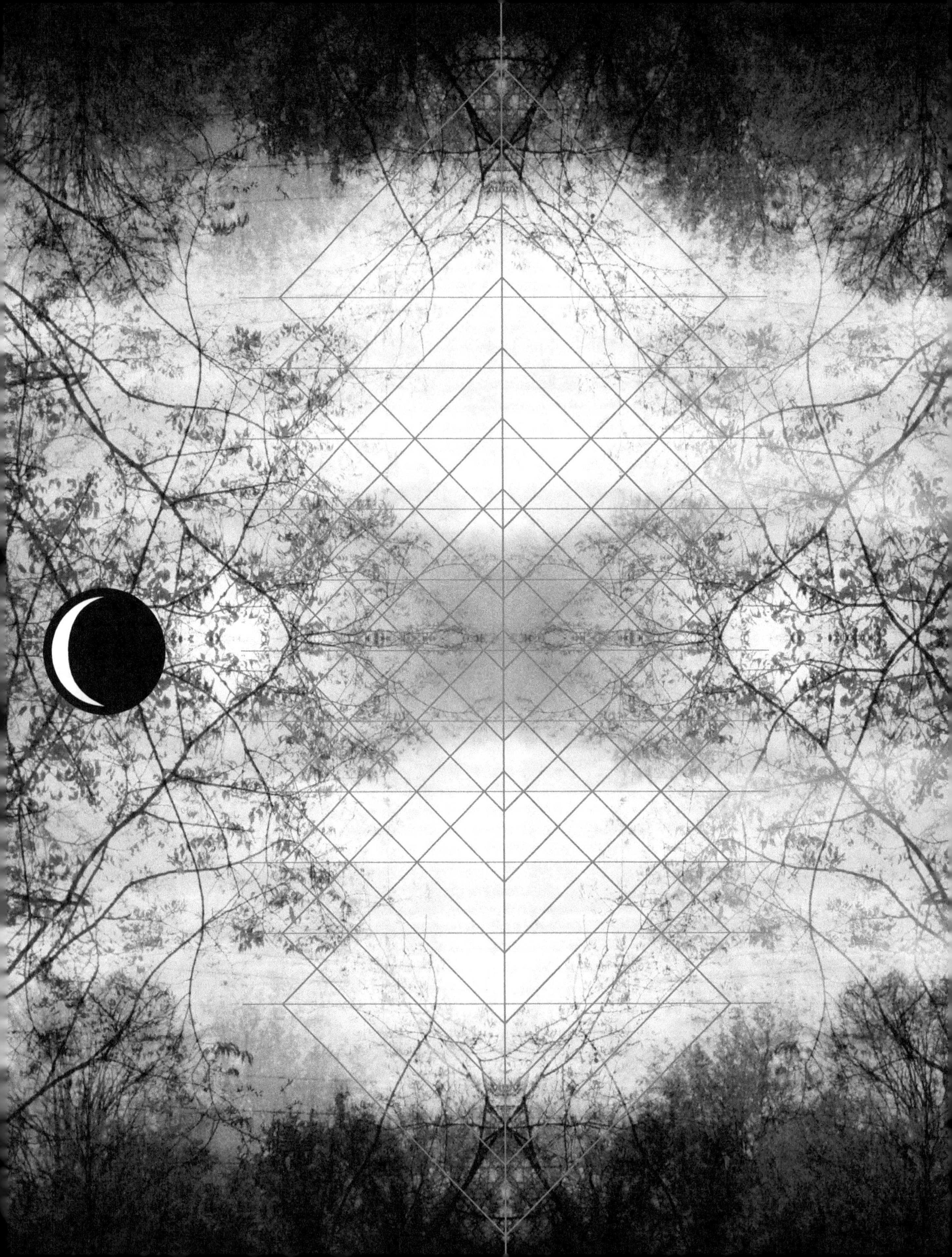

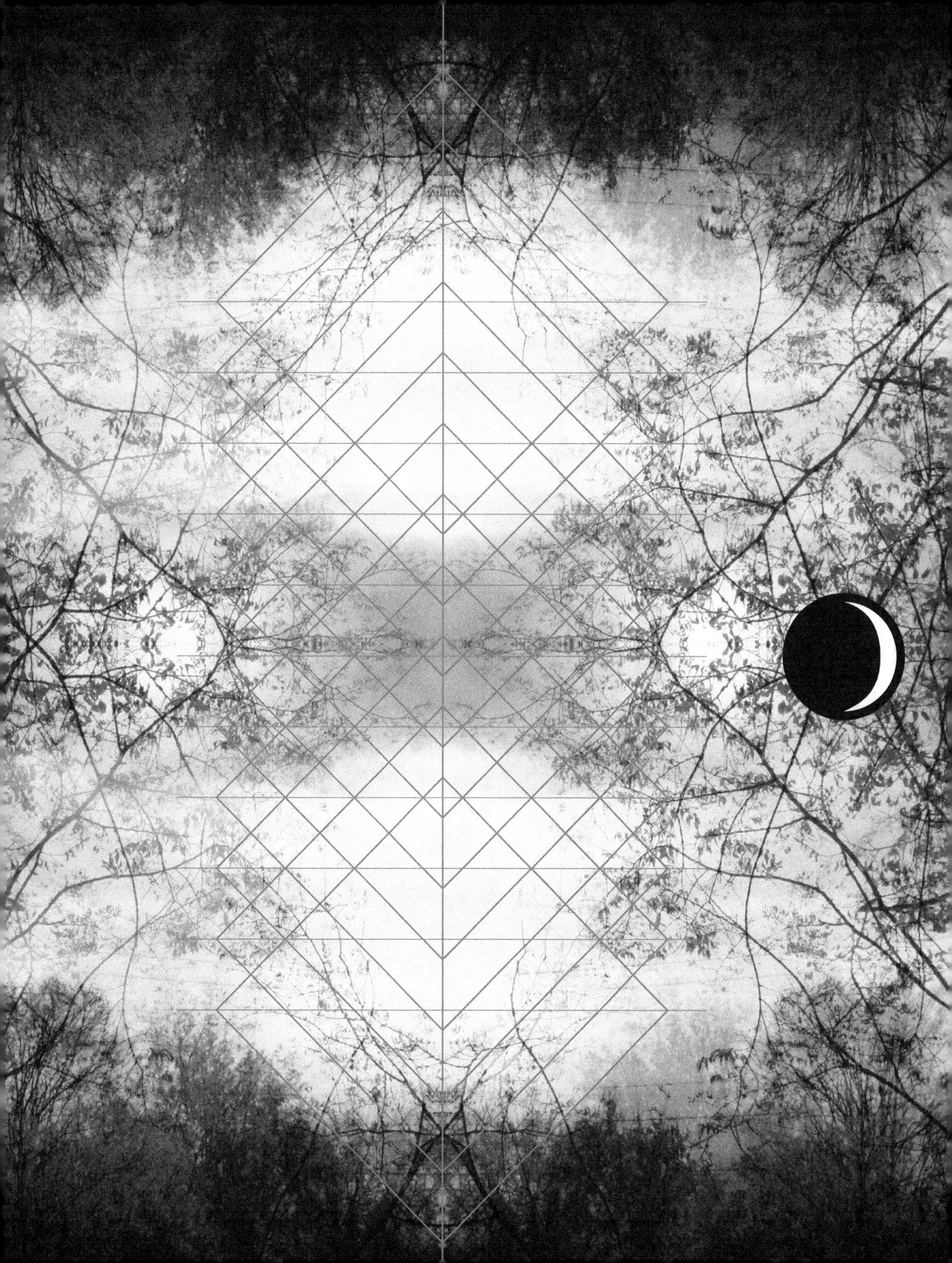

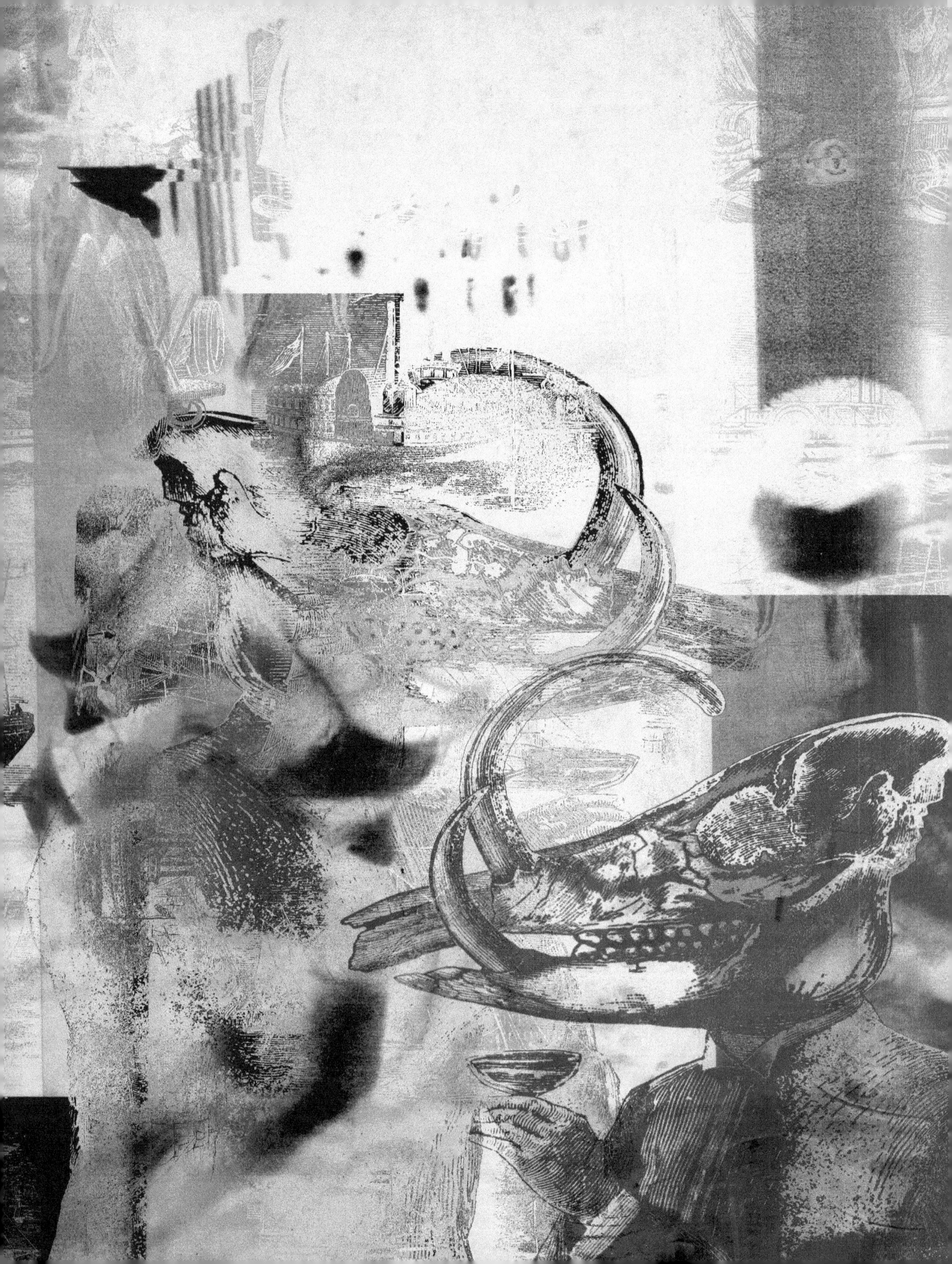

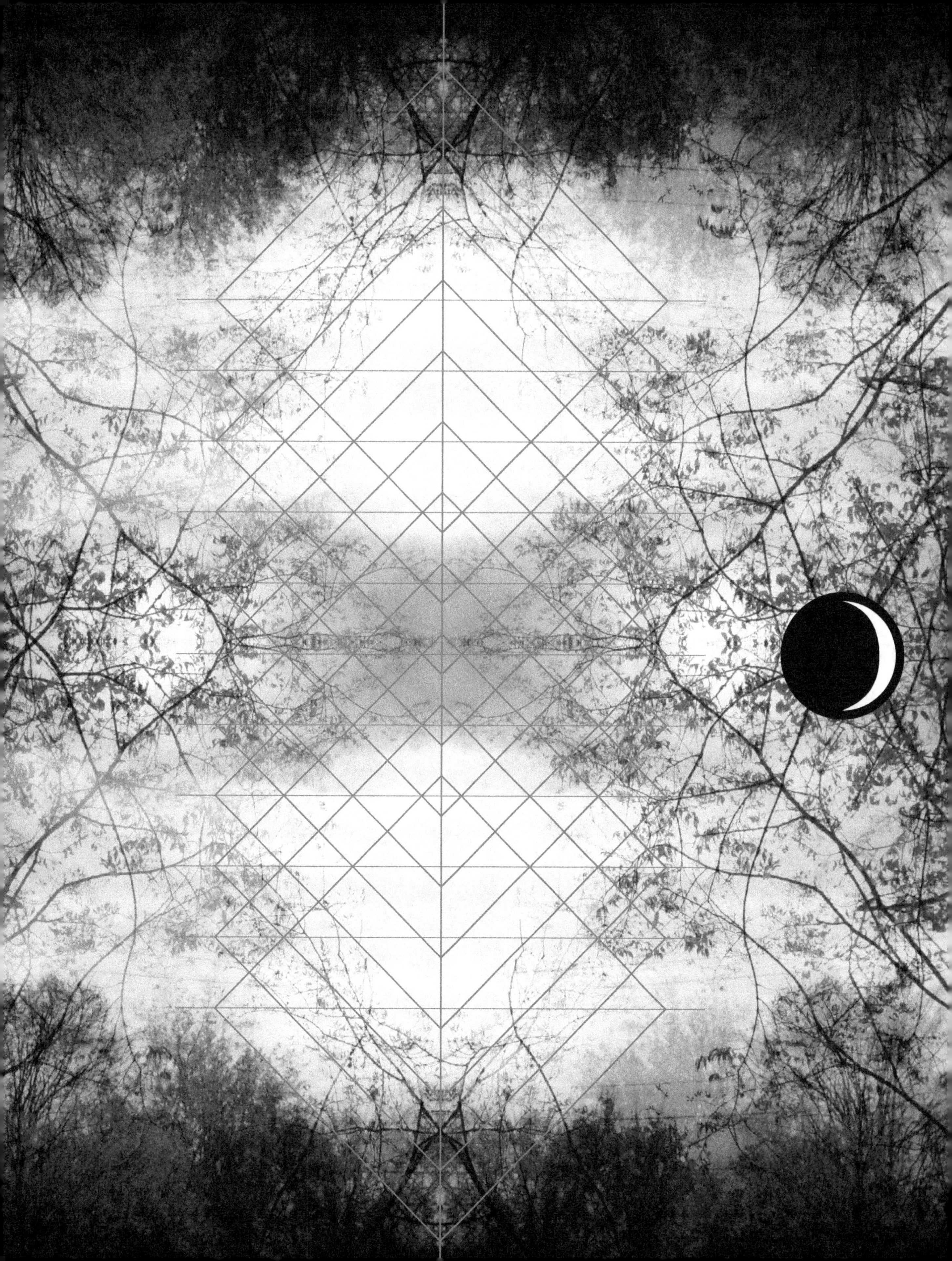

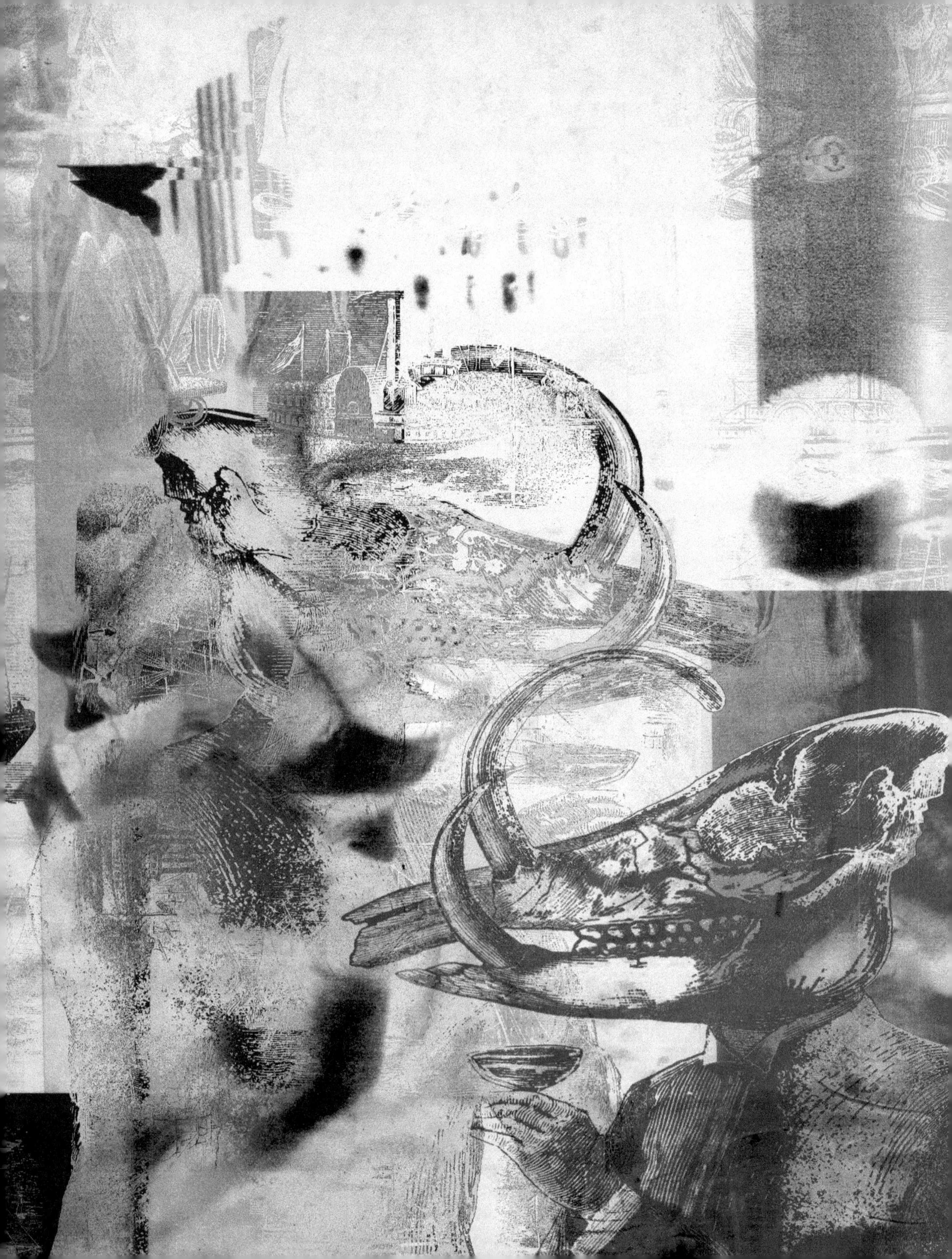

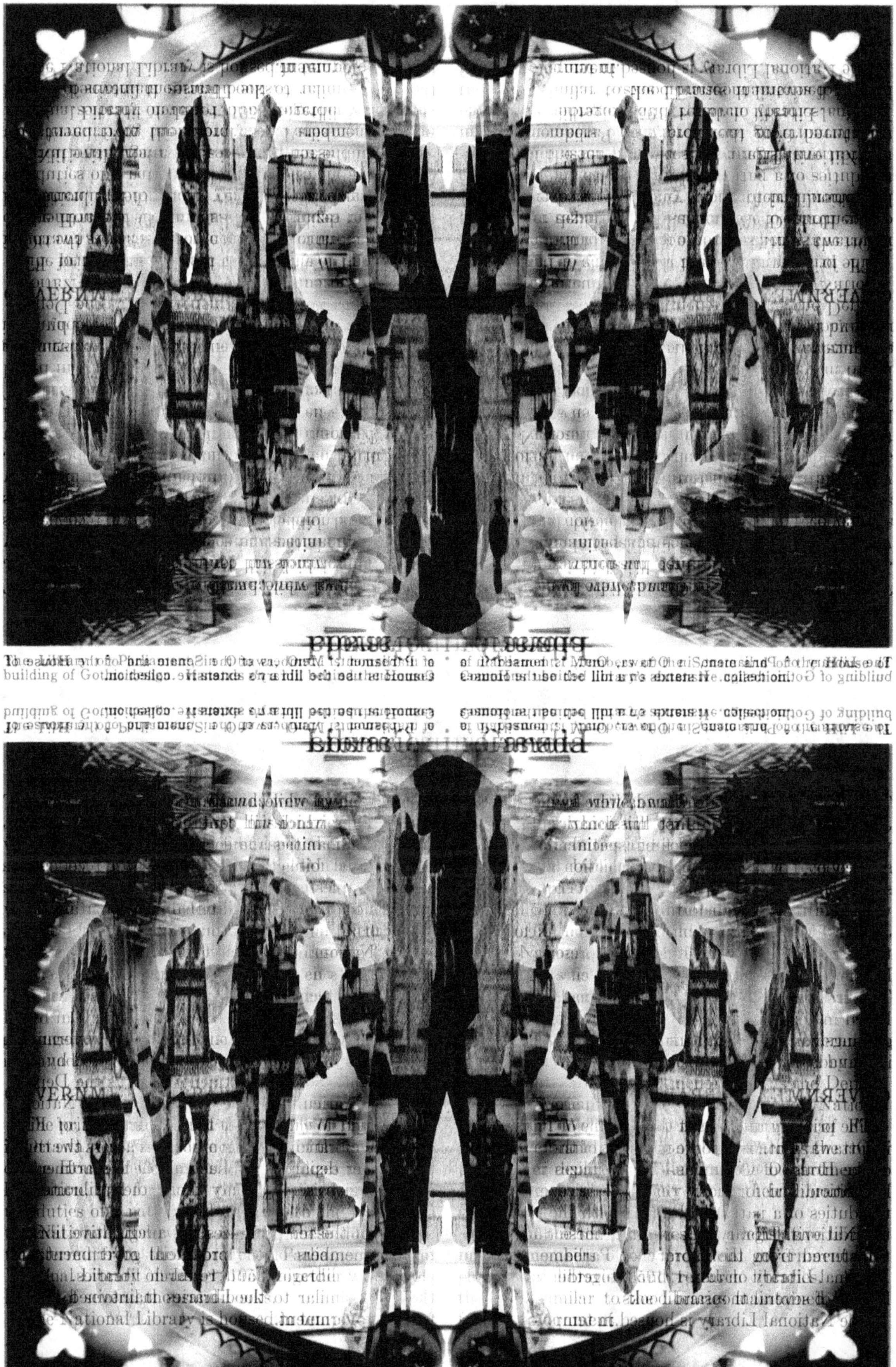

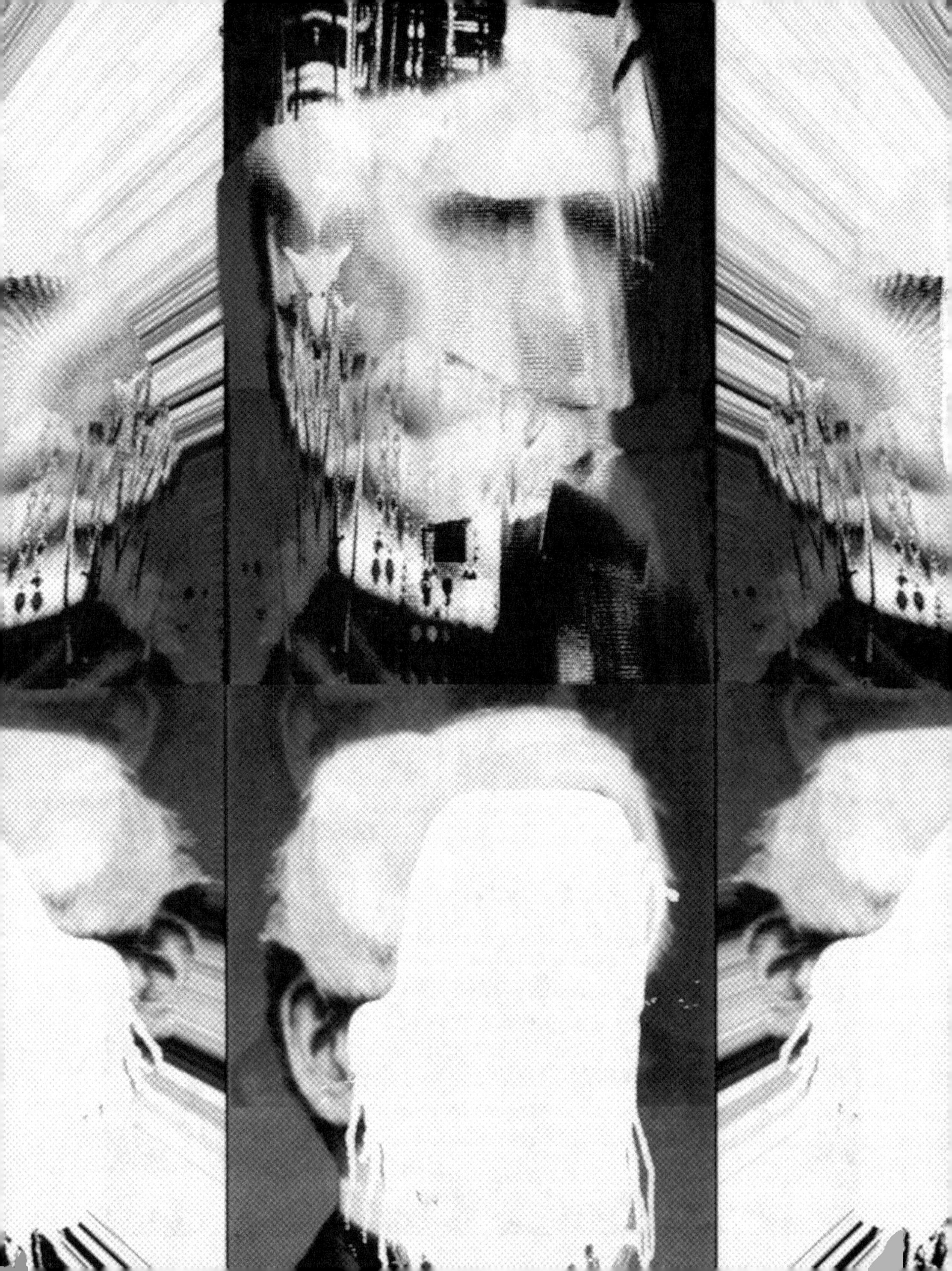

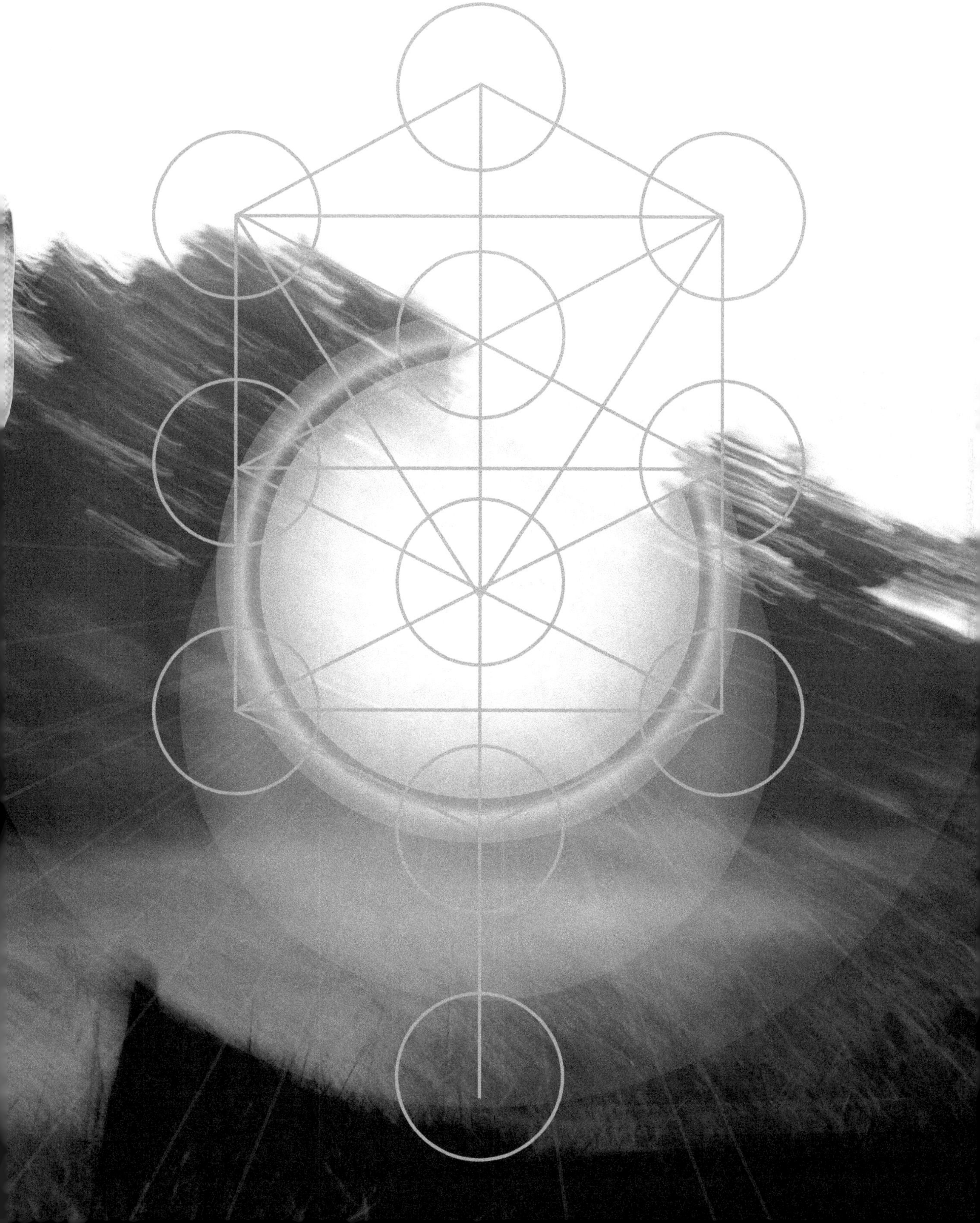

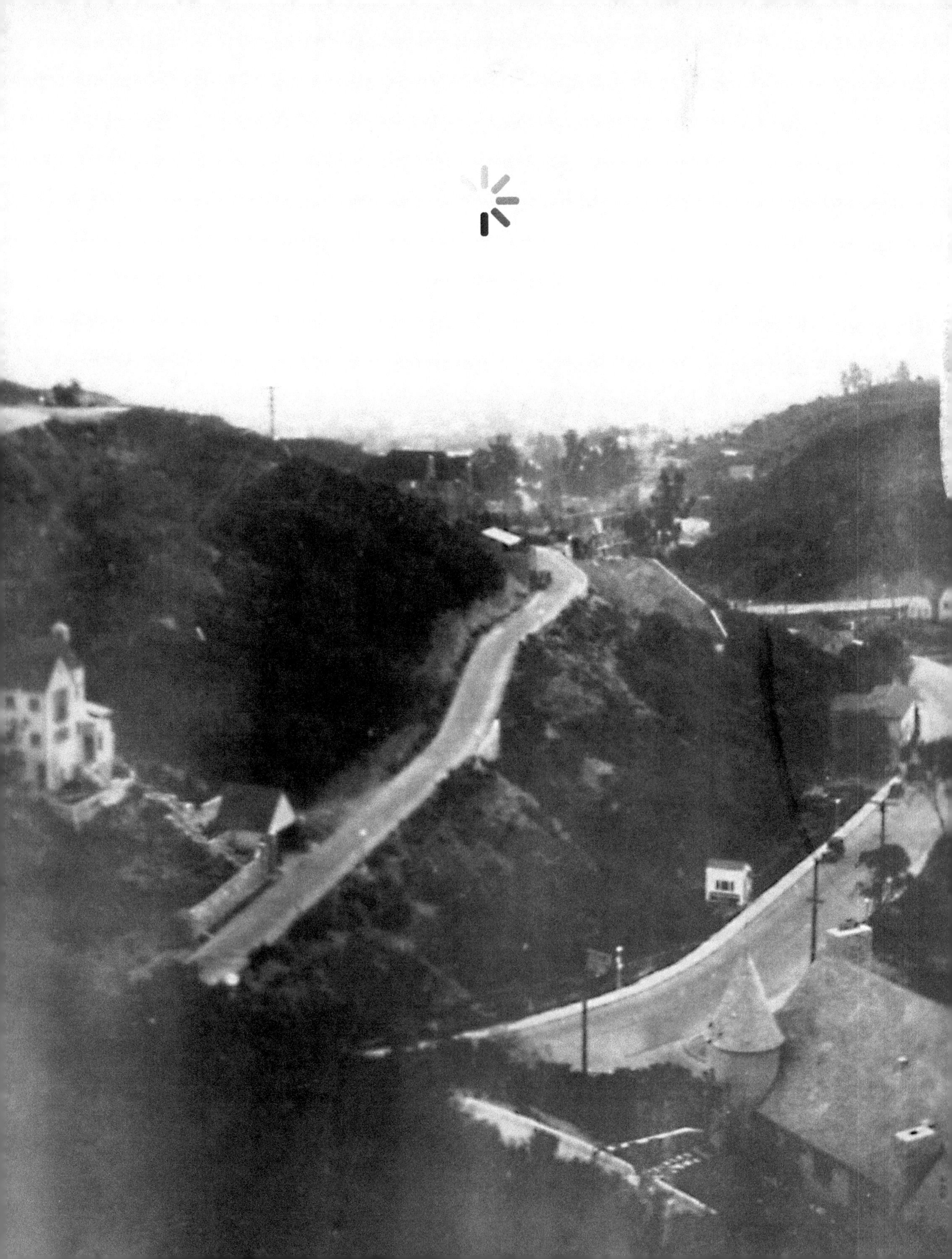

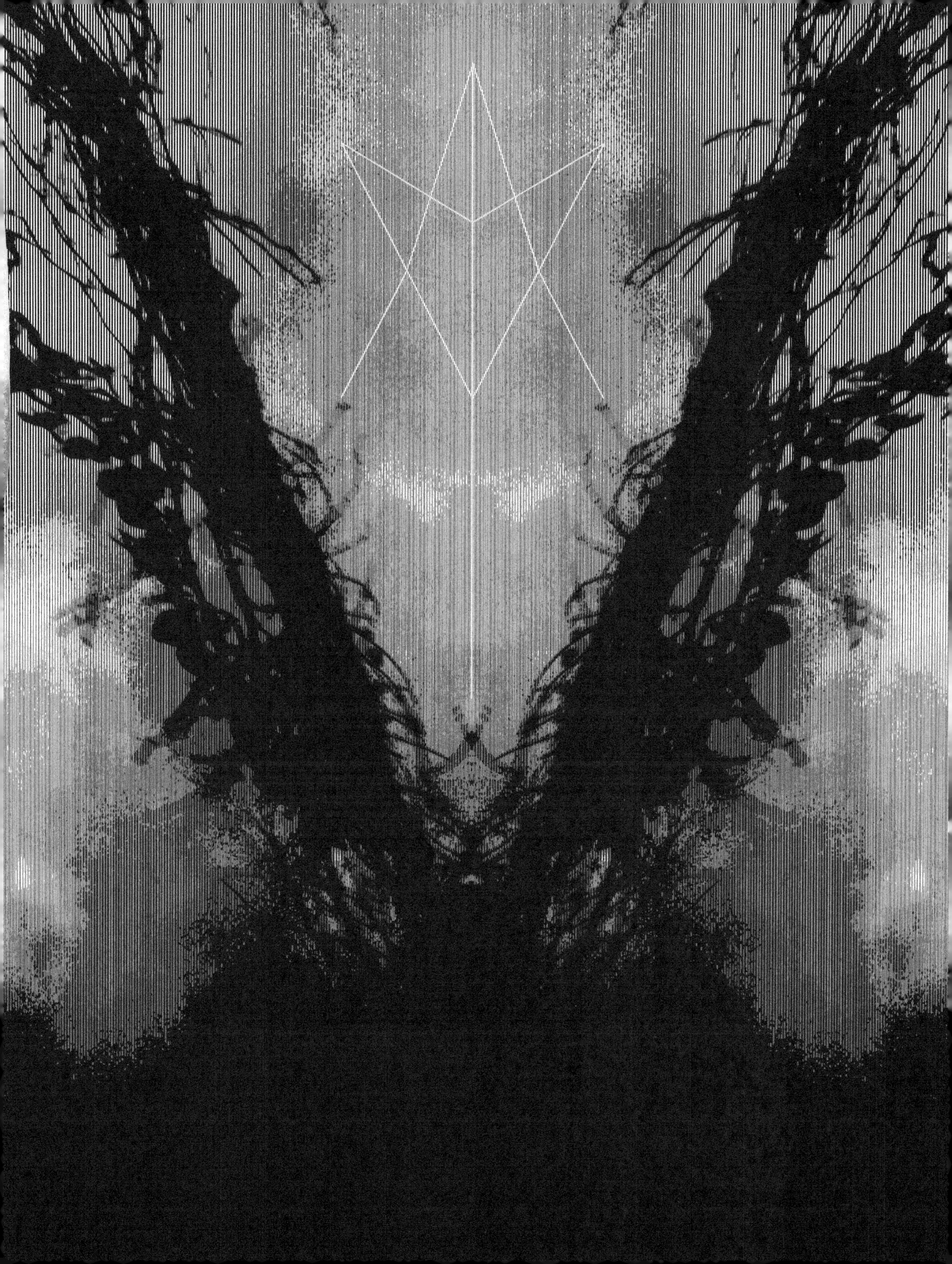

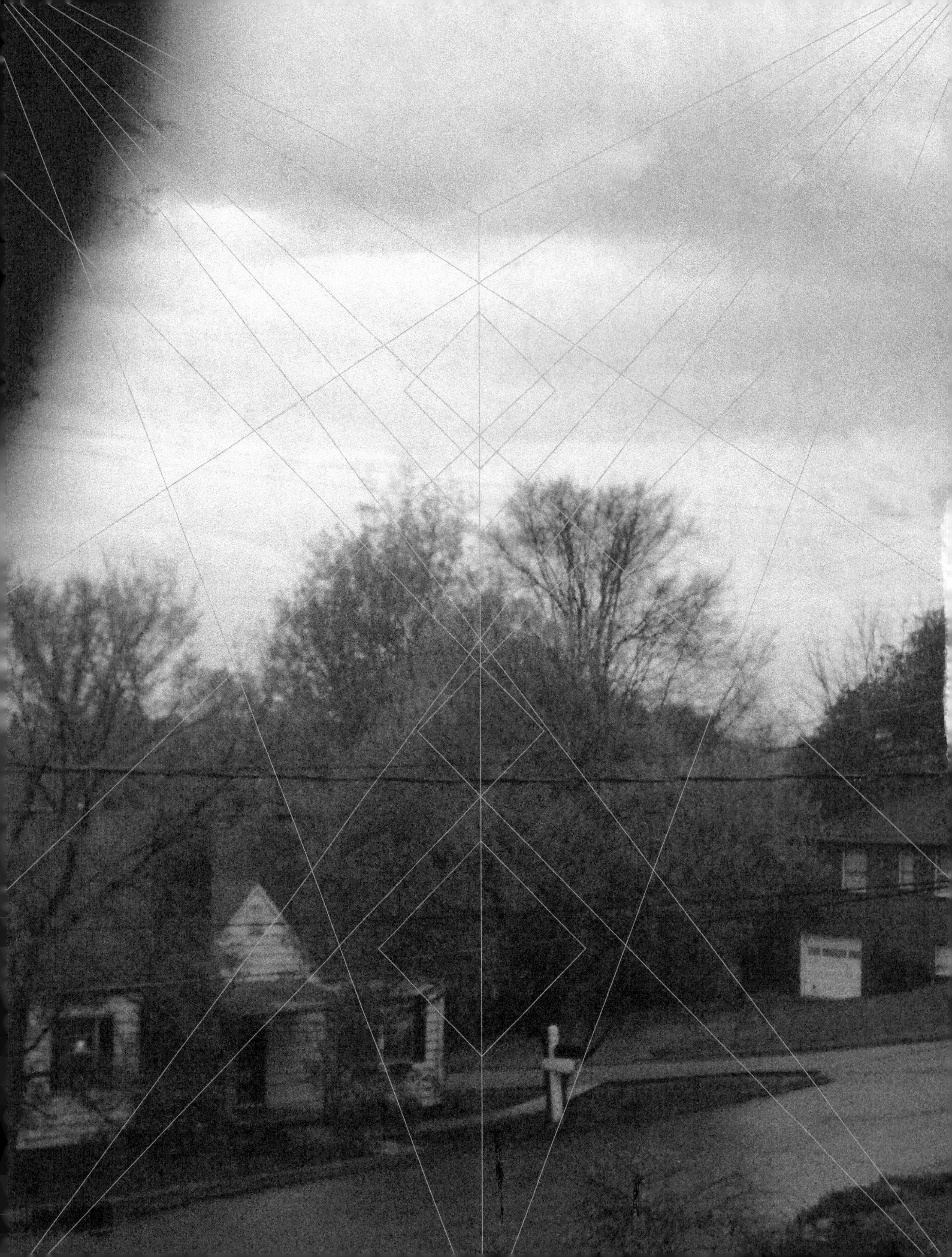

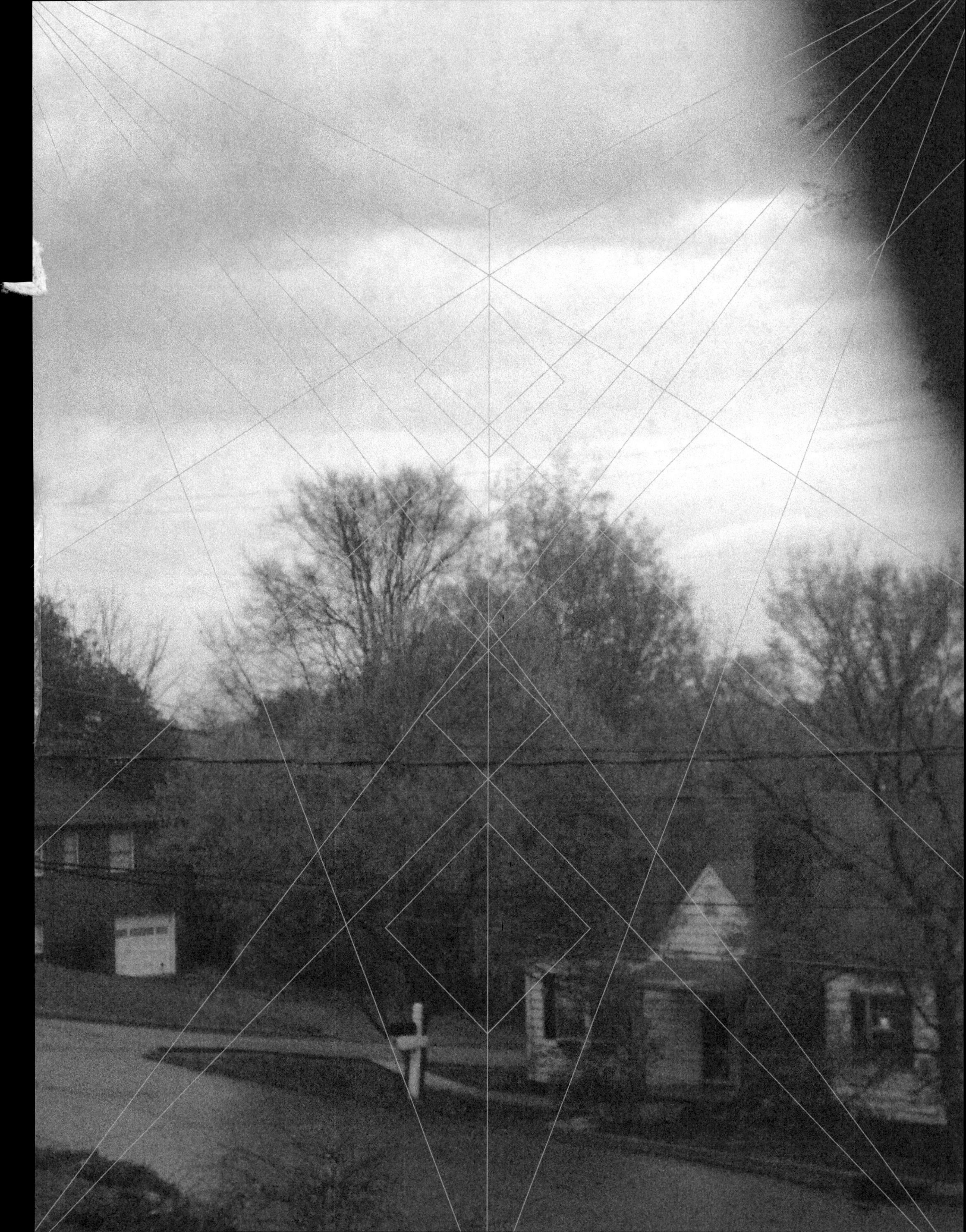

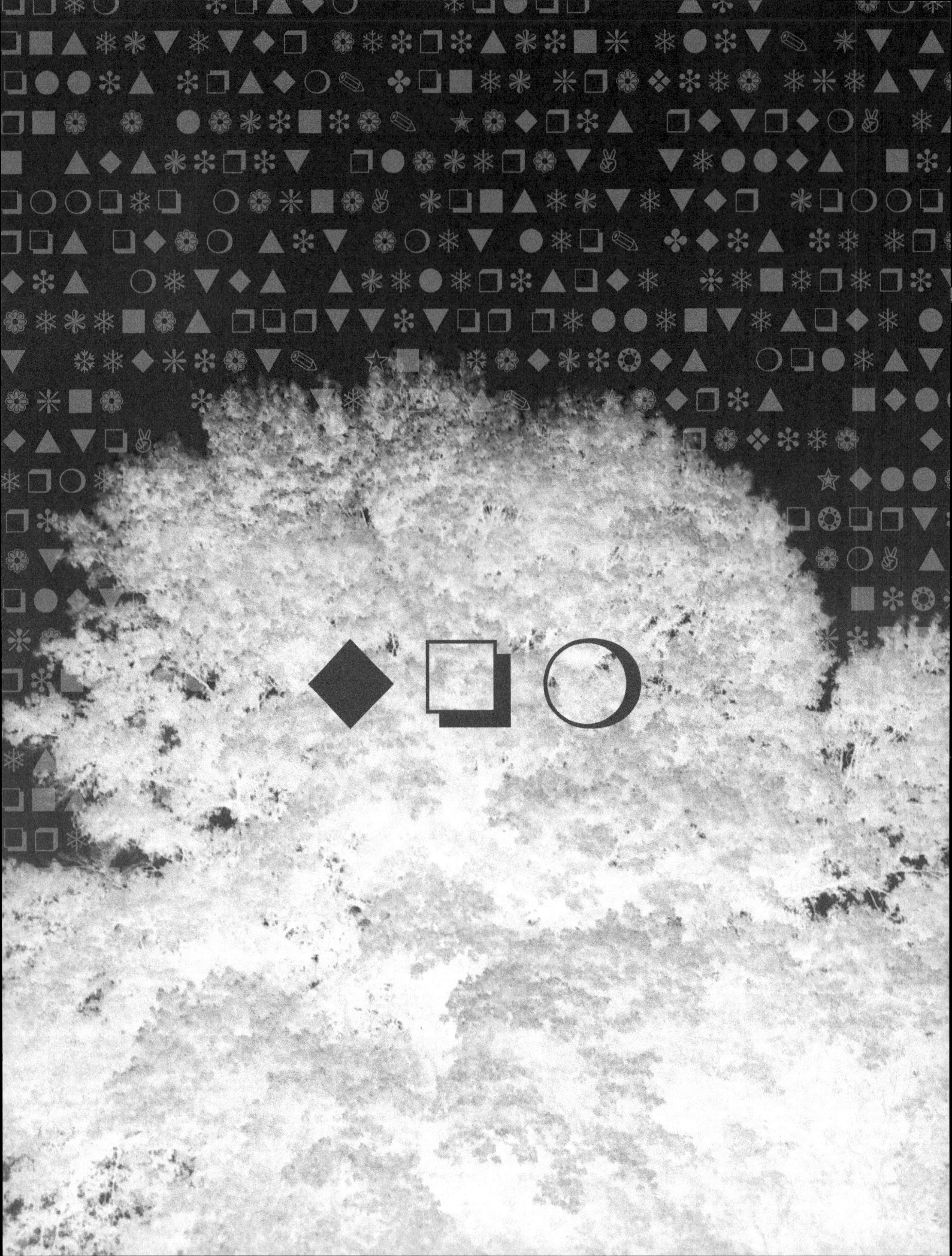

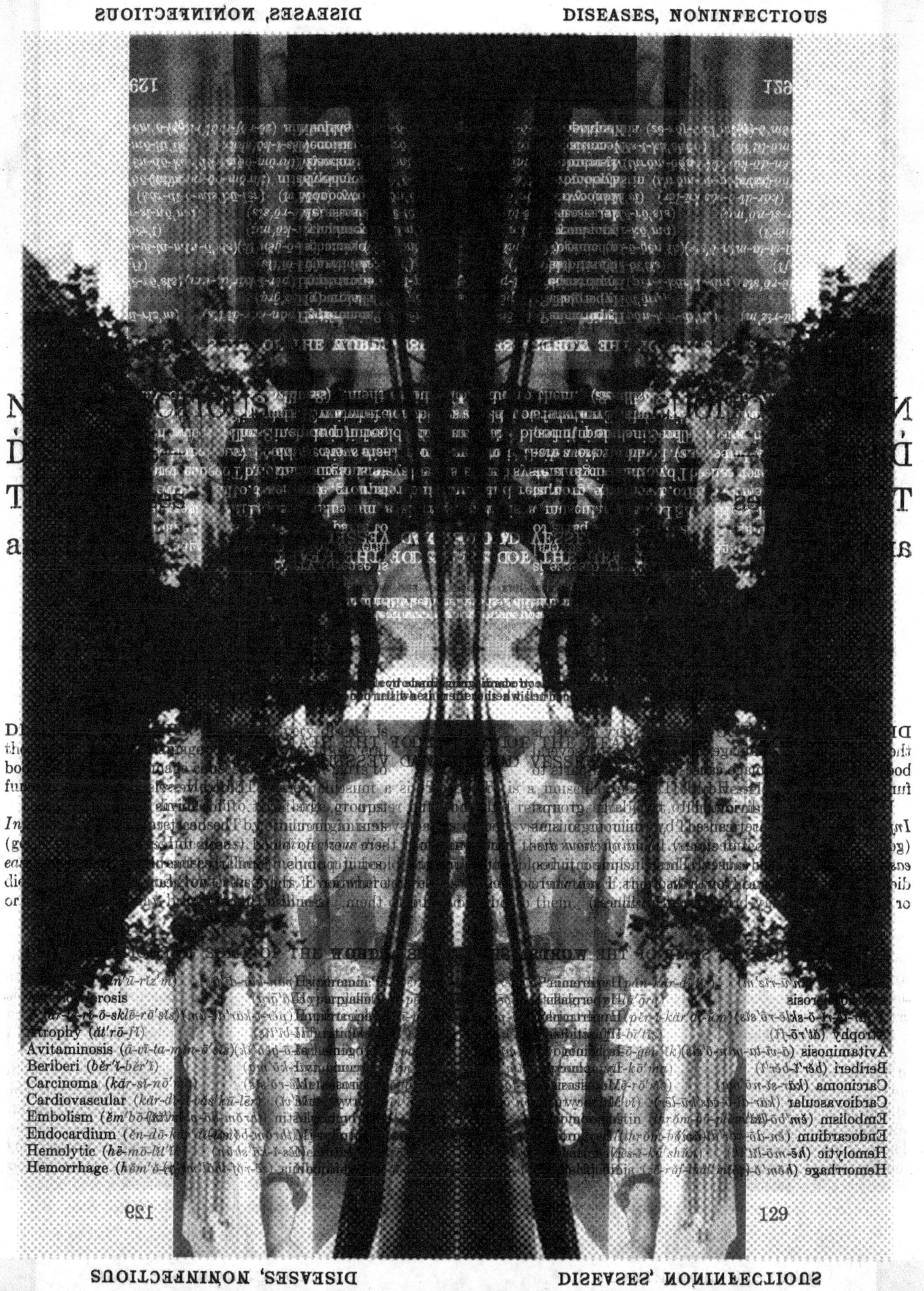
DISEASES, NONINFECTIOUS
Atrophy (ăt'rō-fĭ)
Avitaminosis
Beriberi
Carcinoma
Cardiovascular
Embolism
Endocardium
Hemolytic
Hemorrhage
129

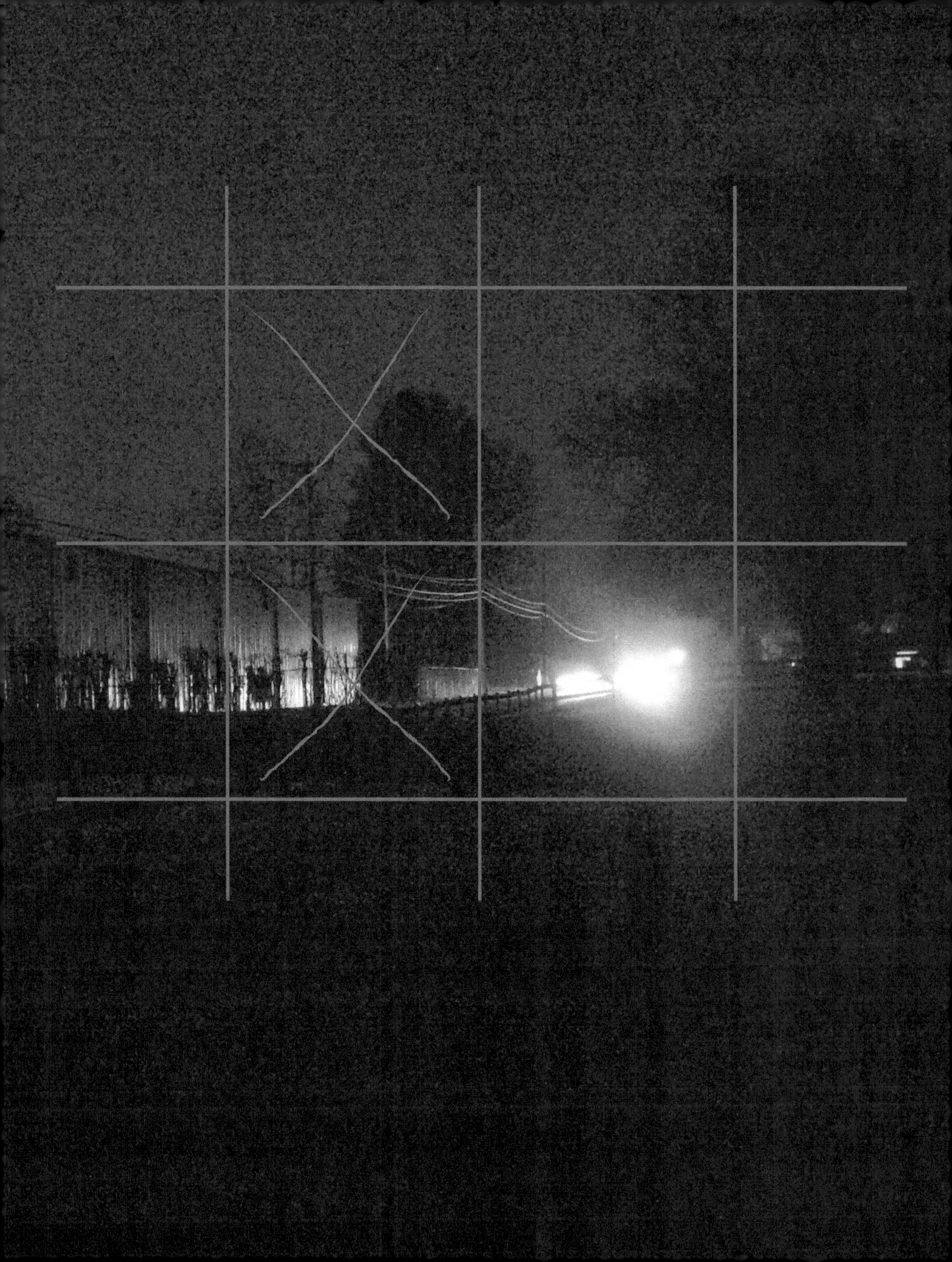

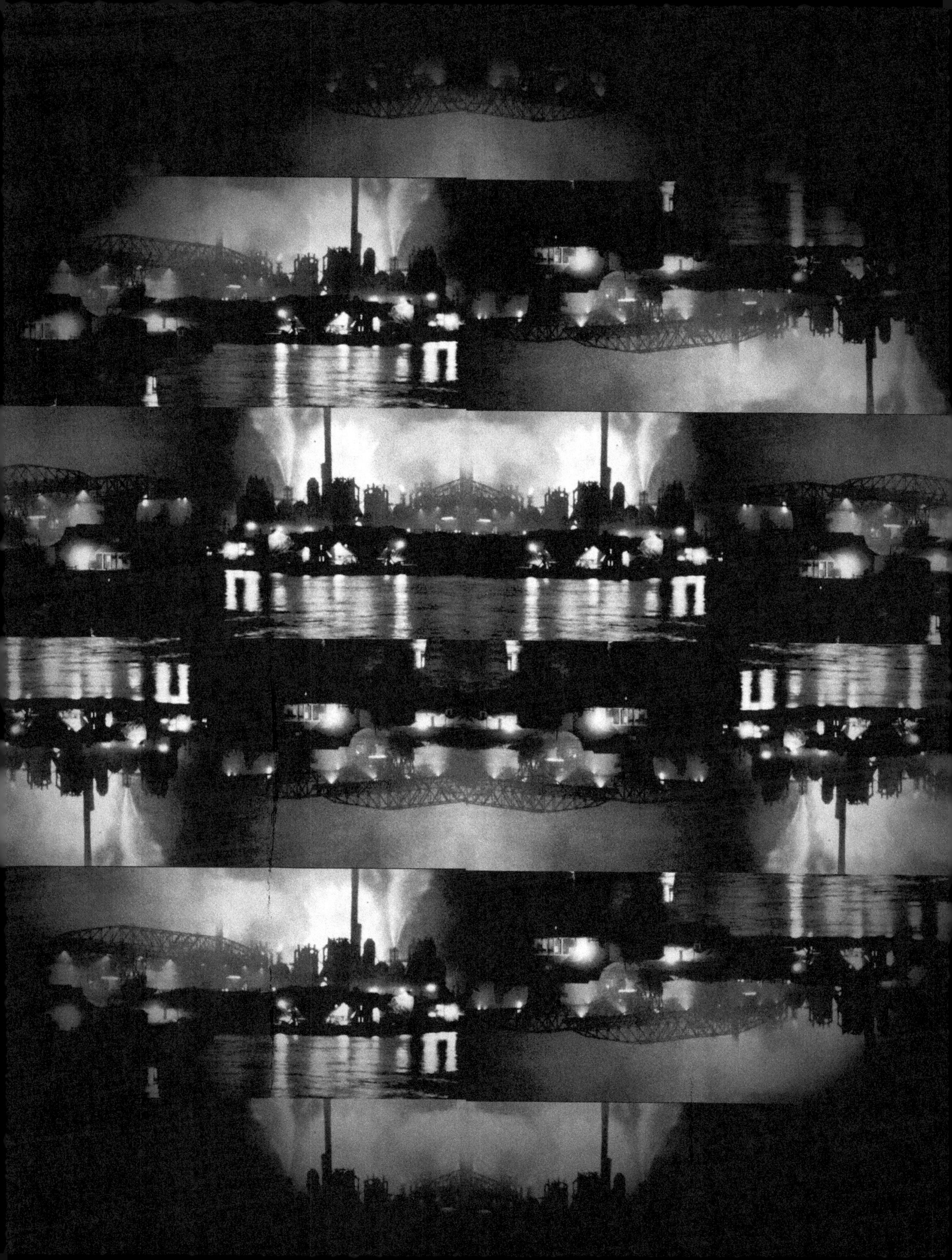

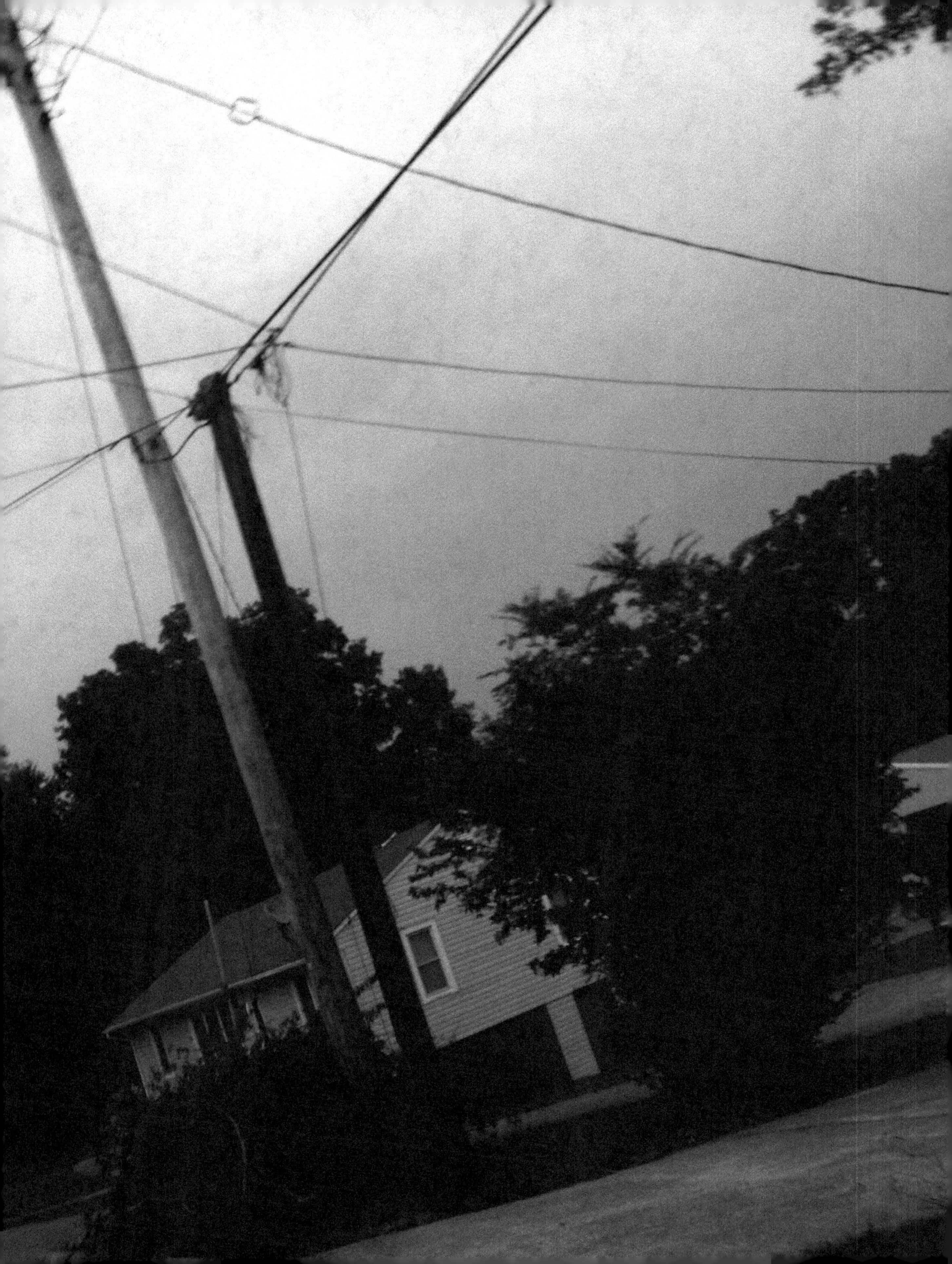

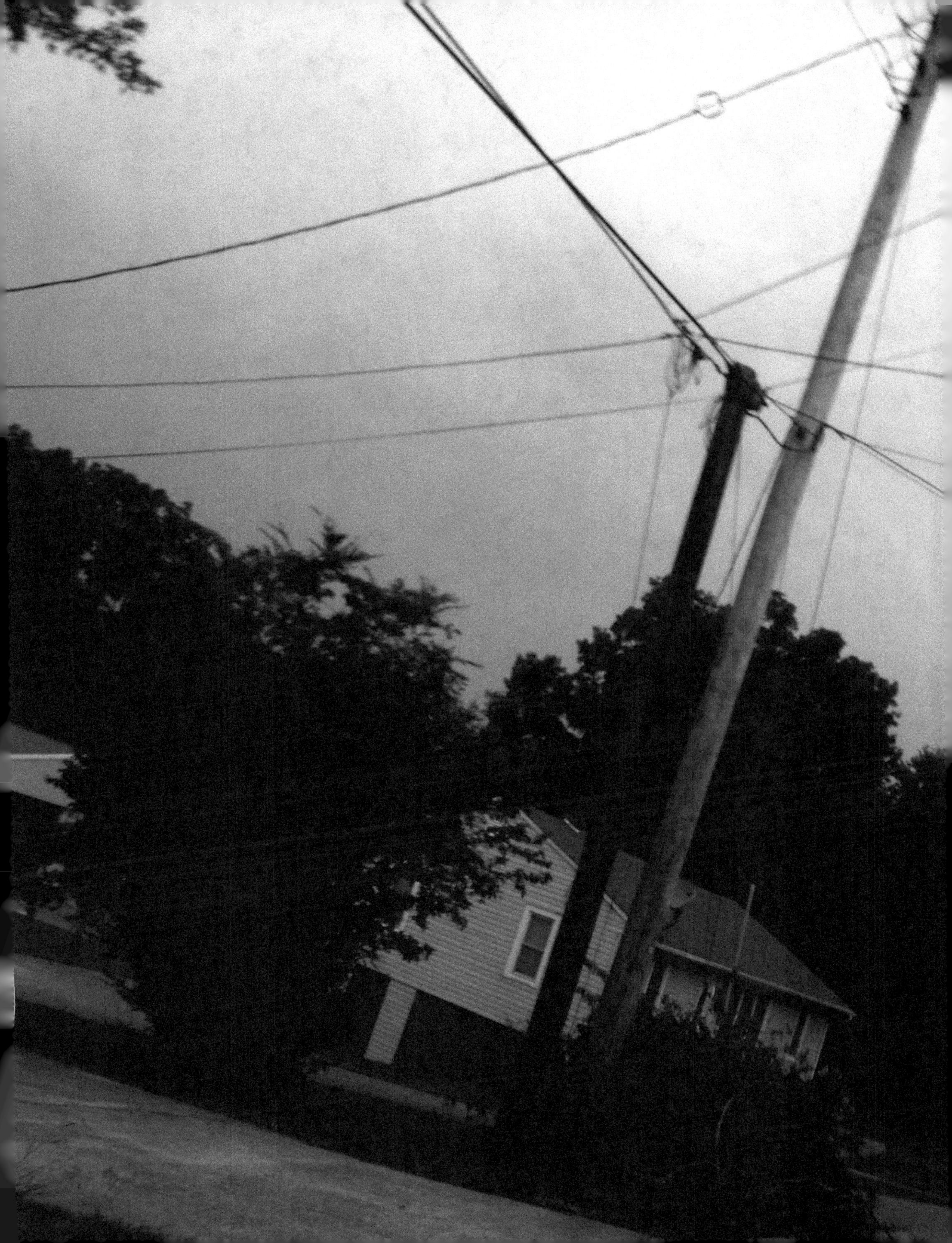

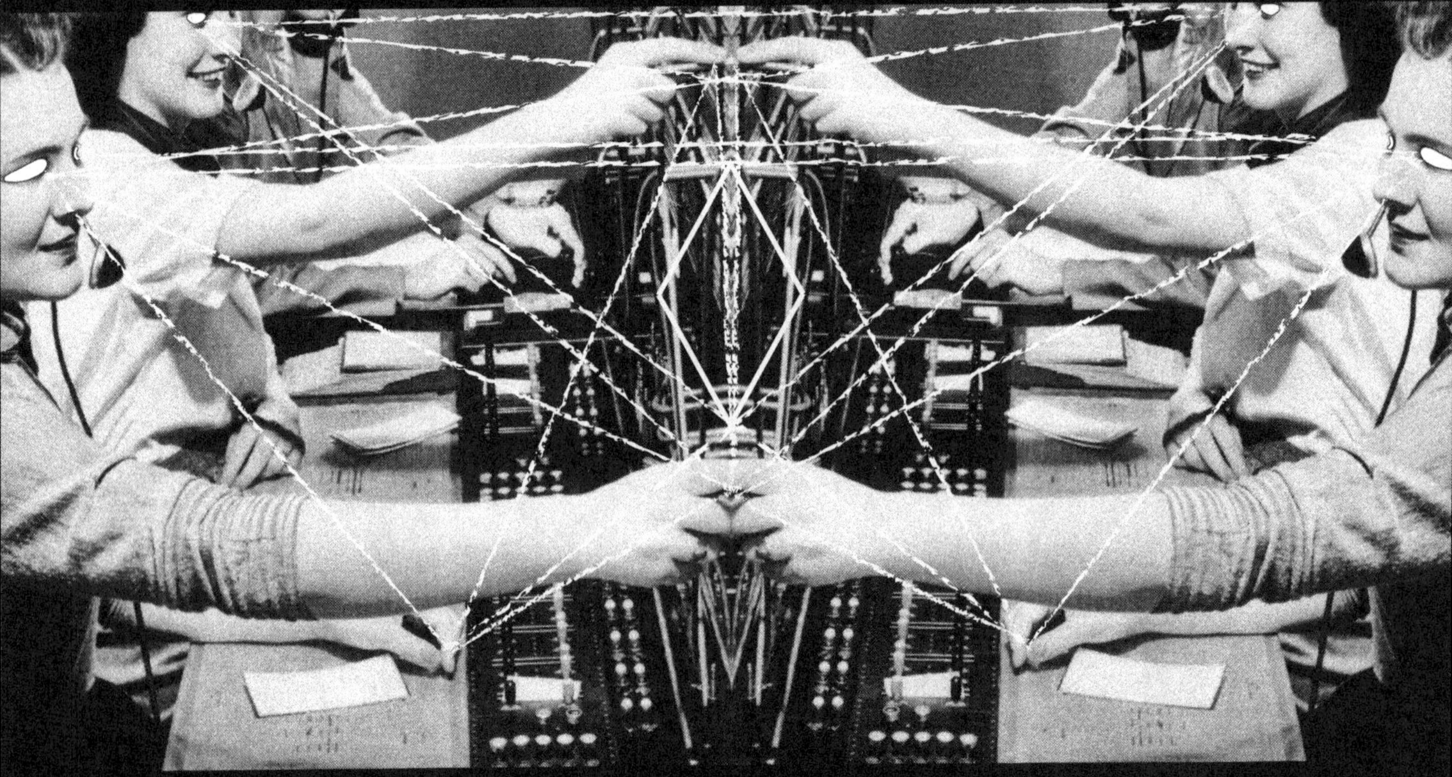

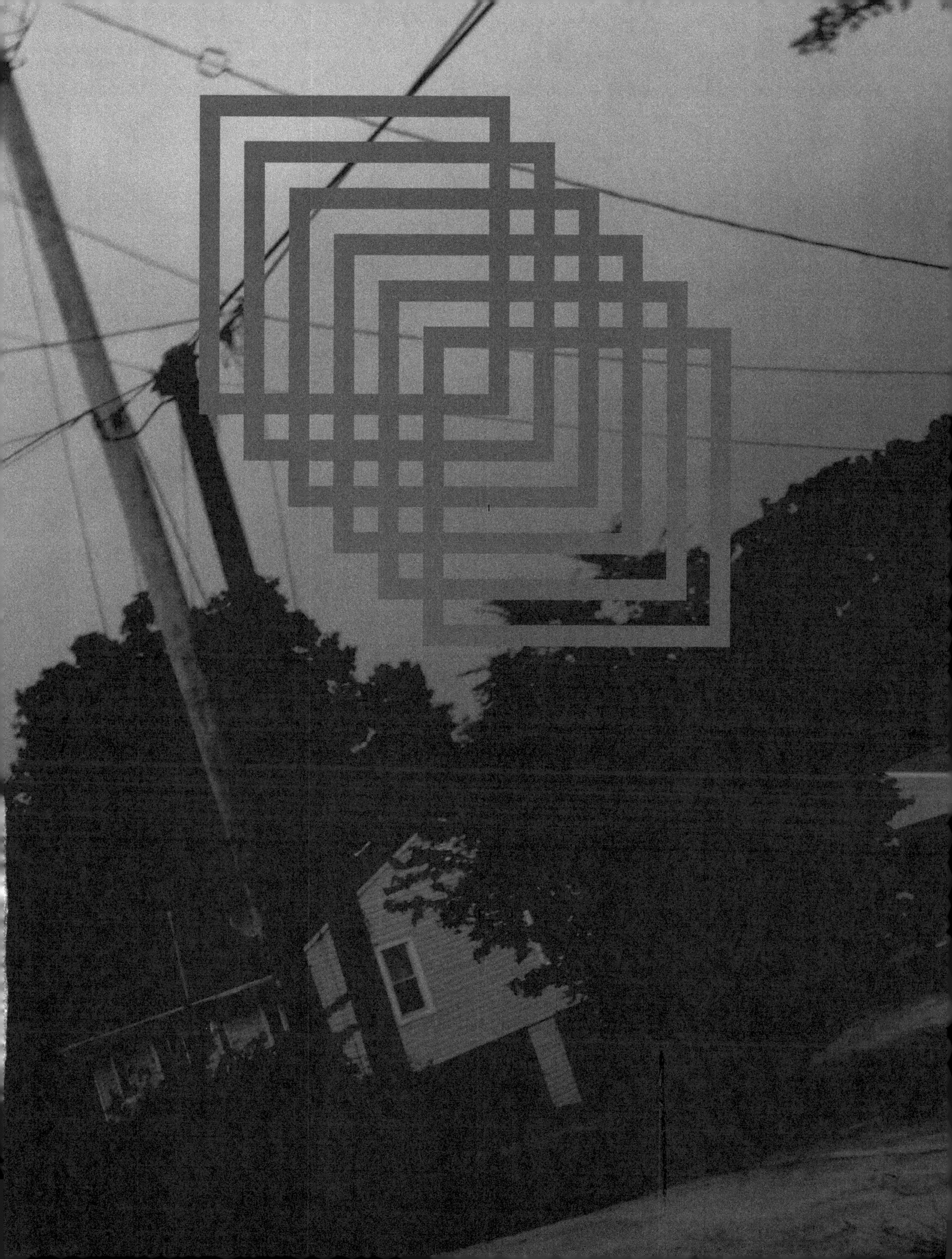

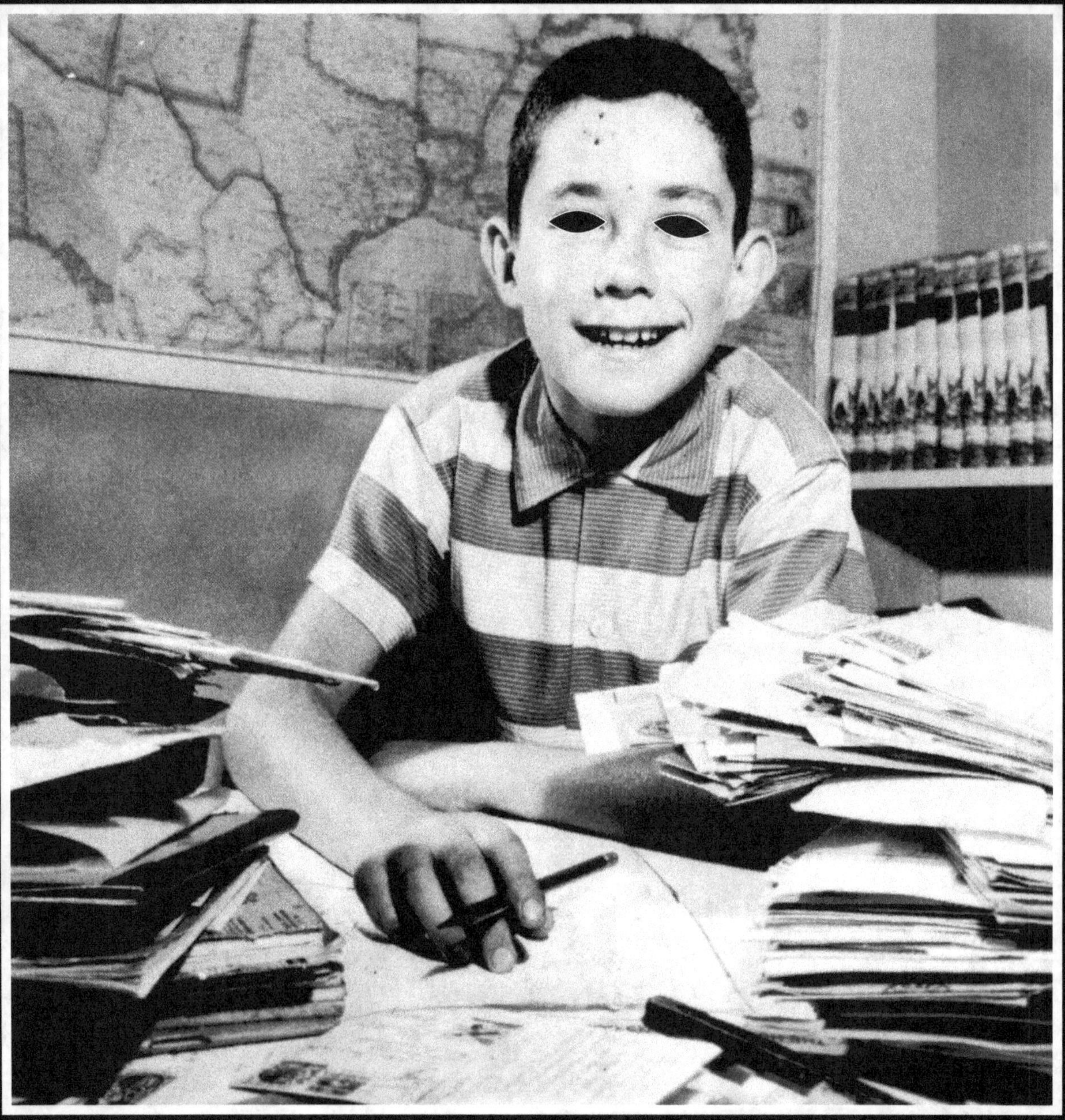

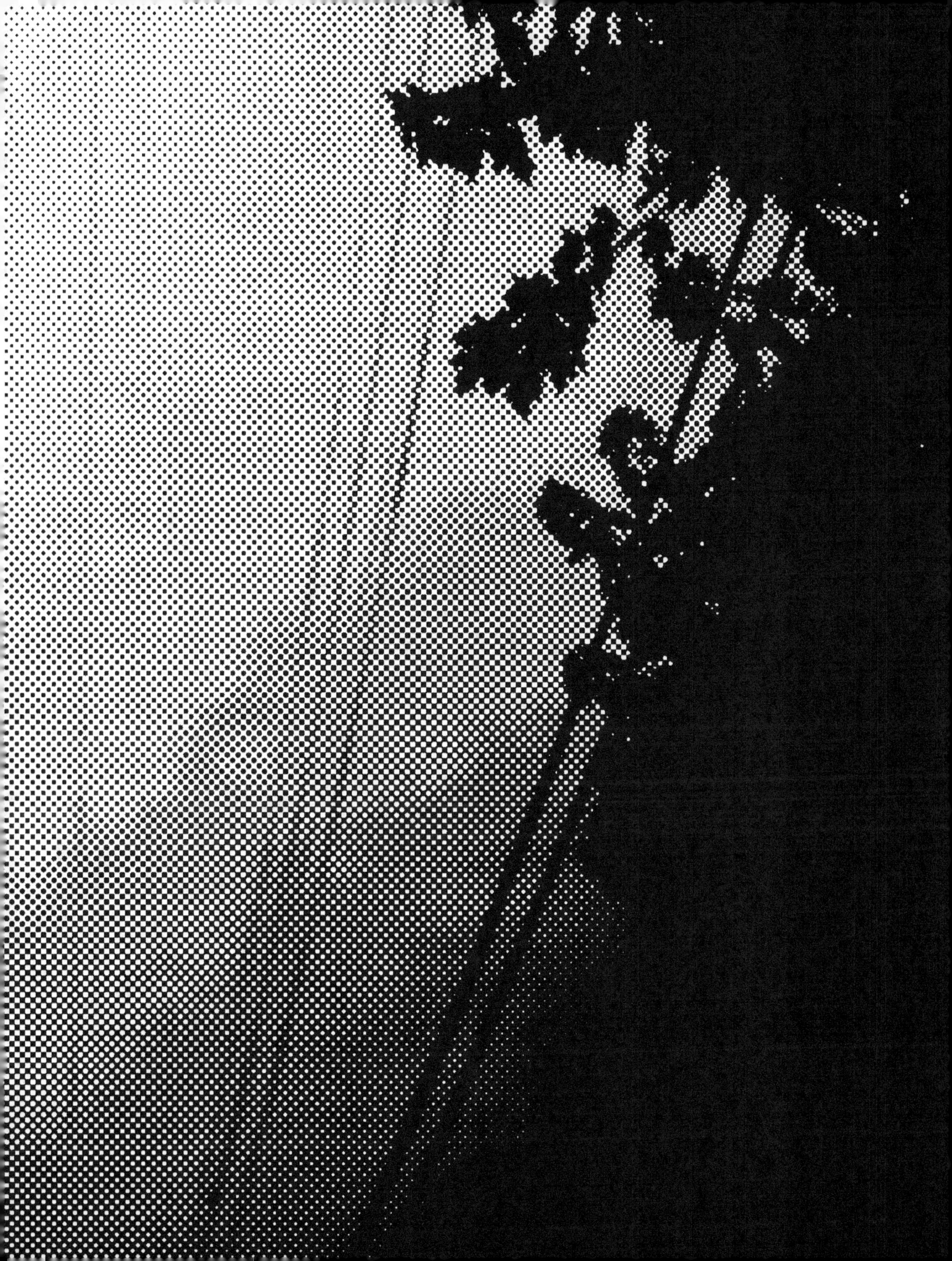

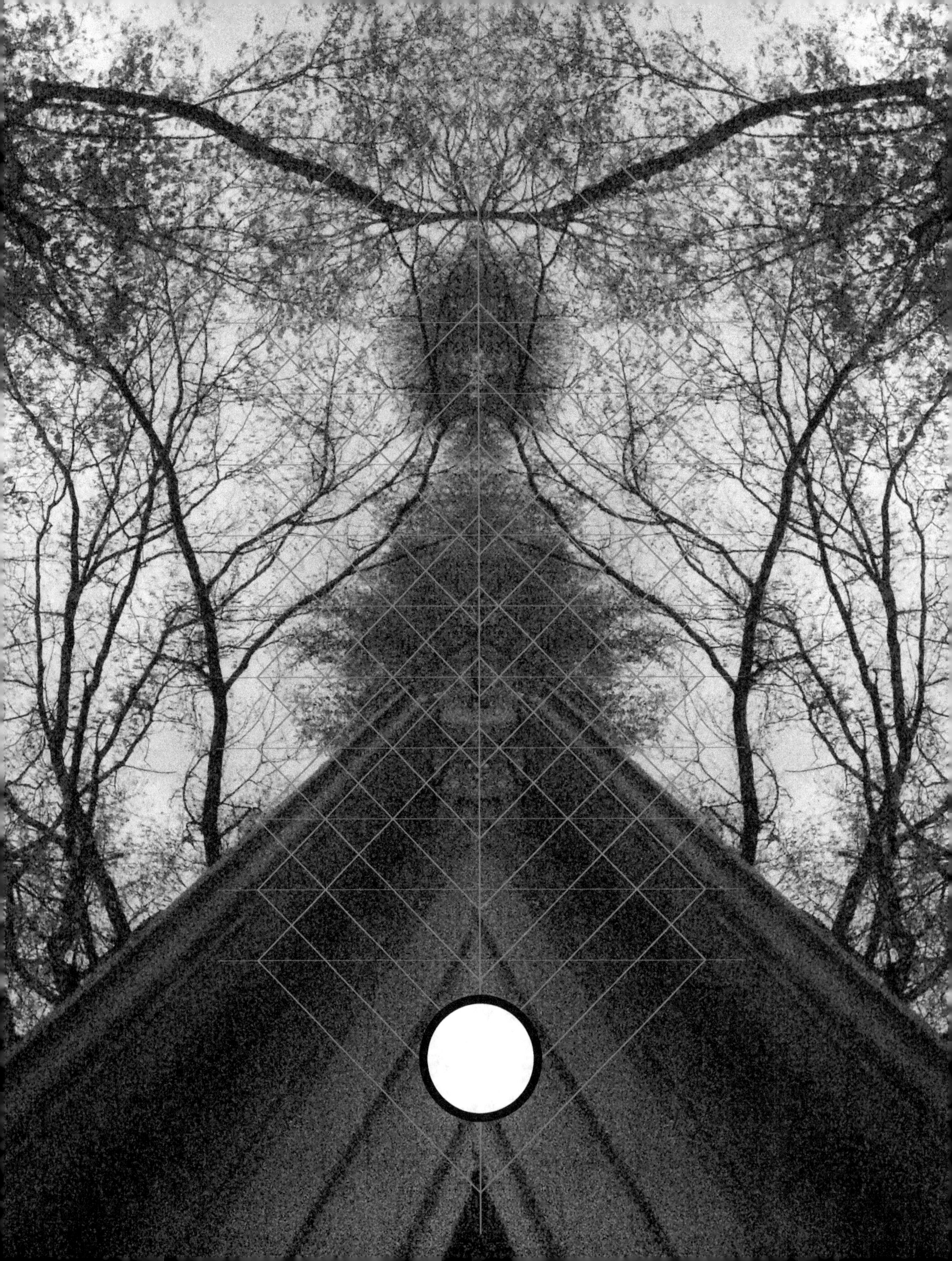

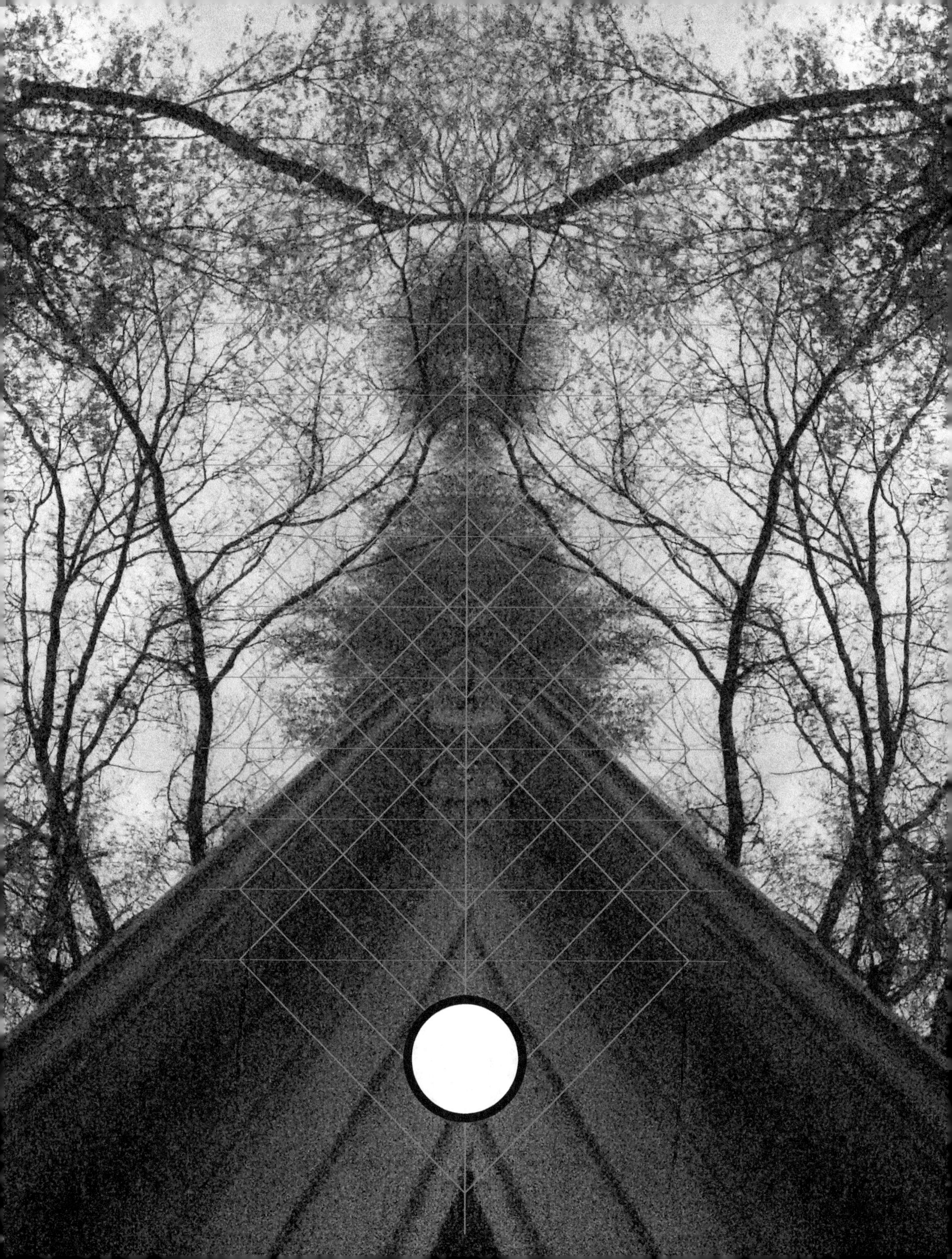

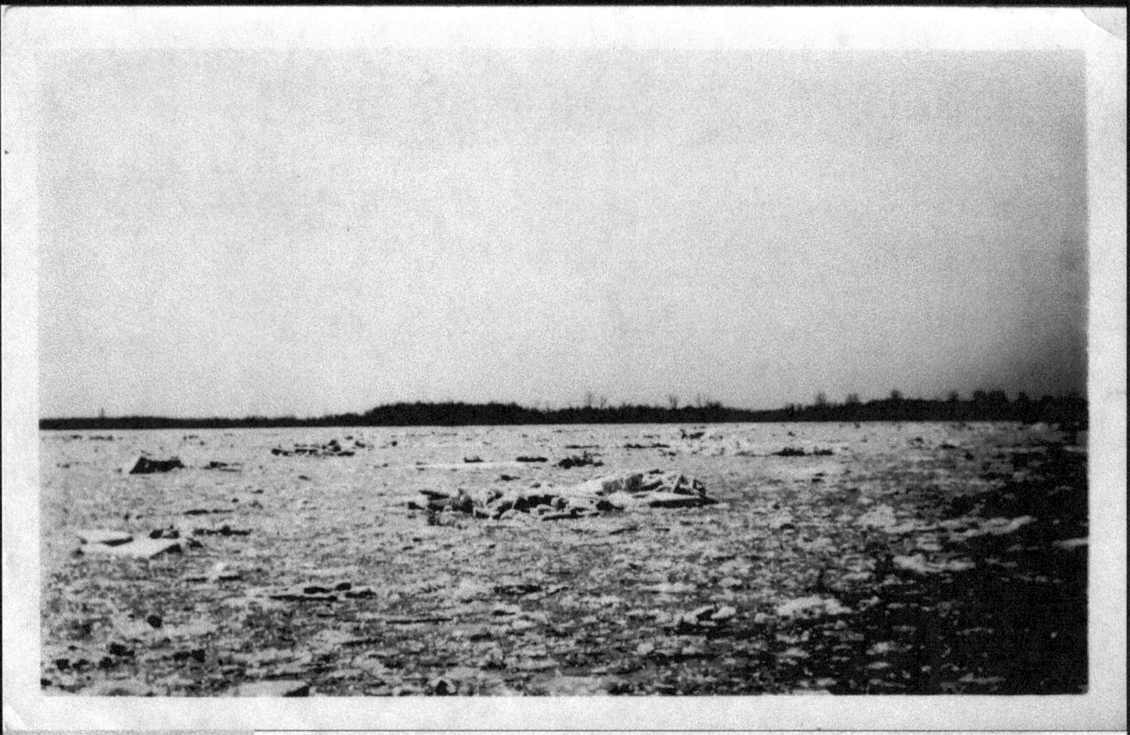

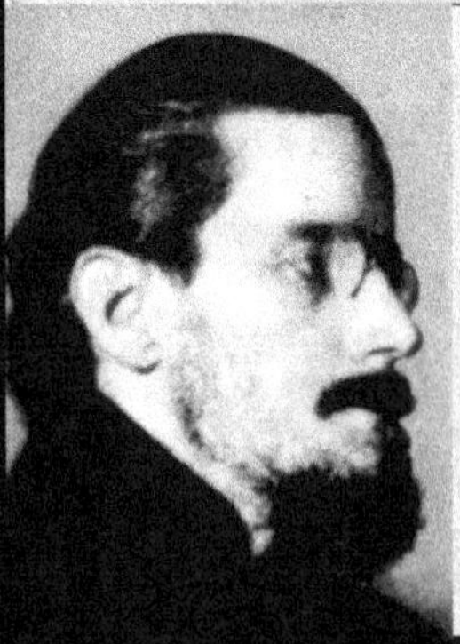

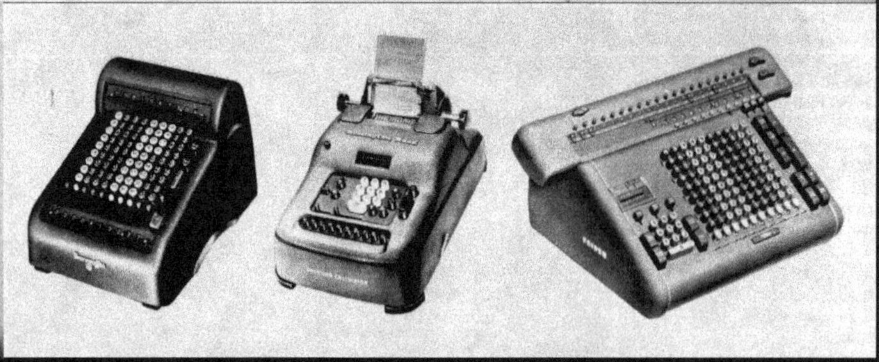

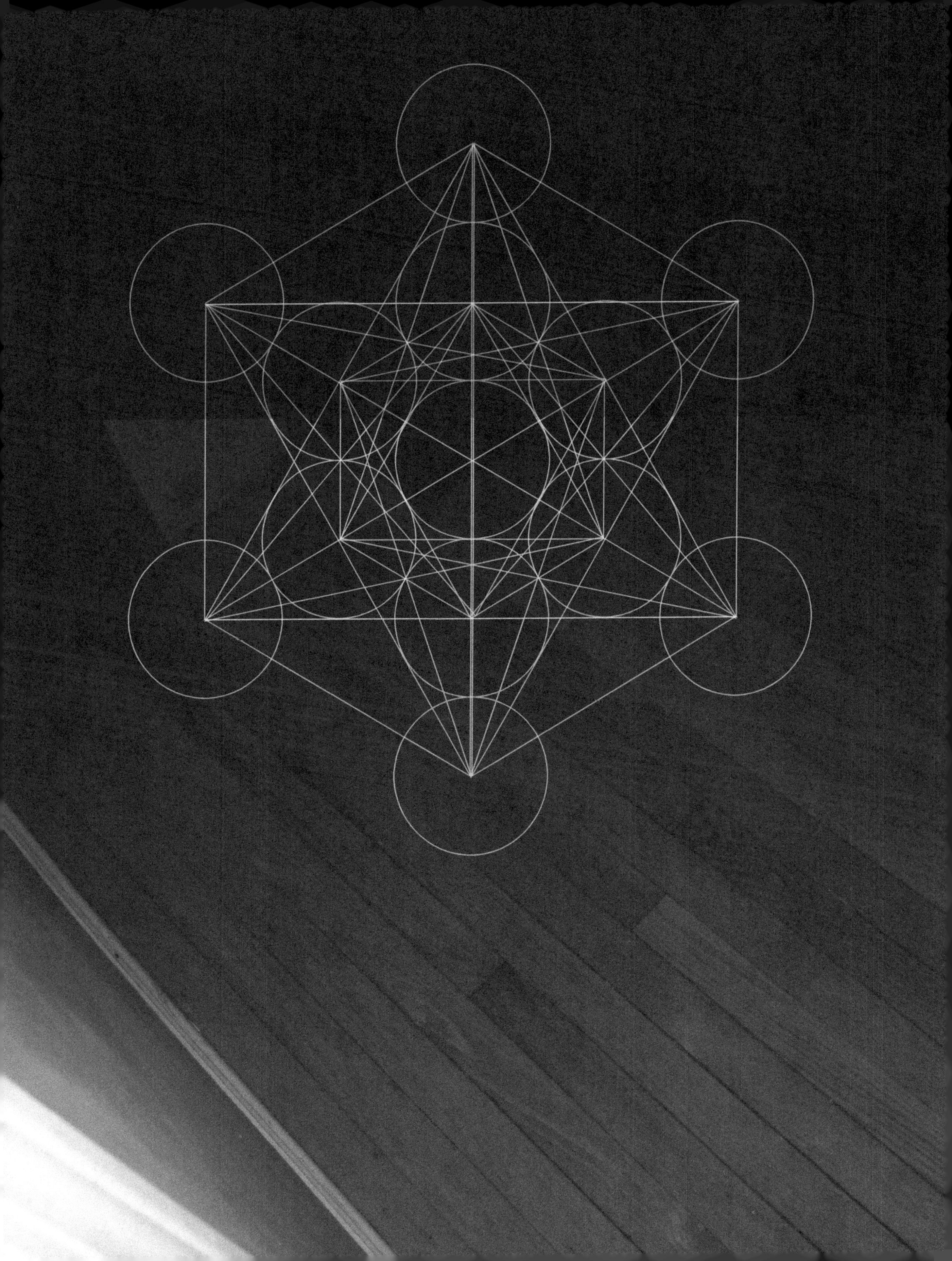

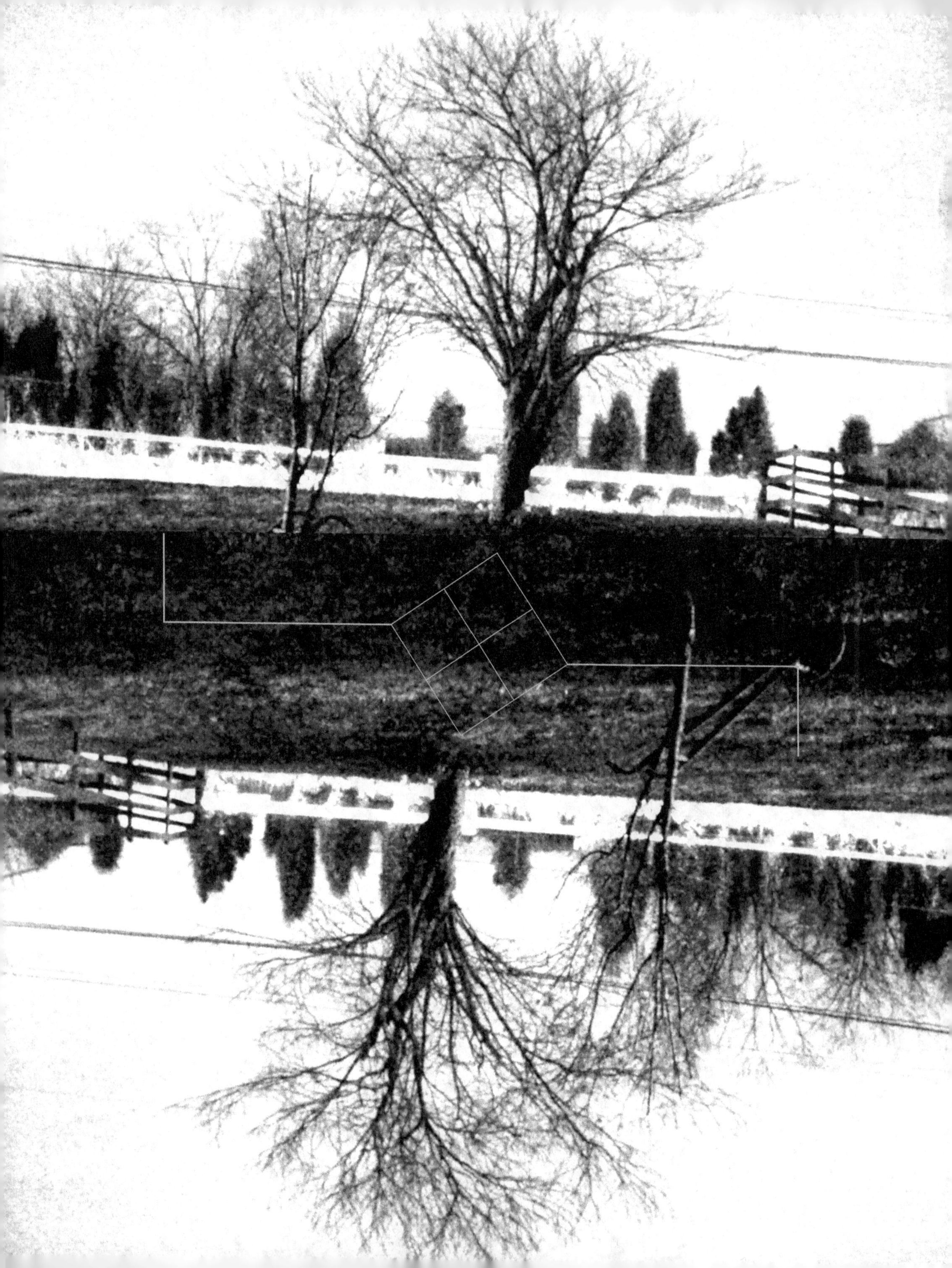

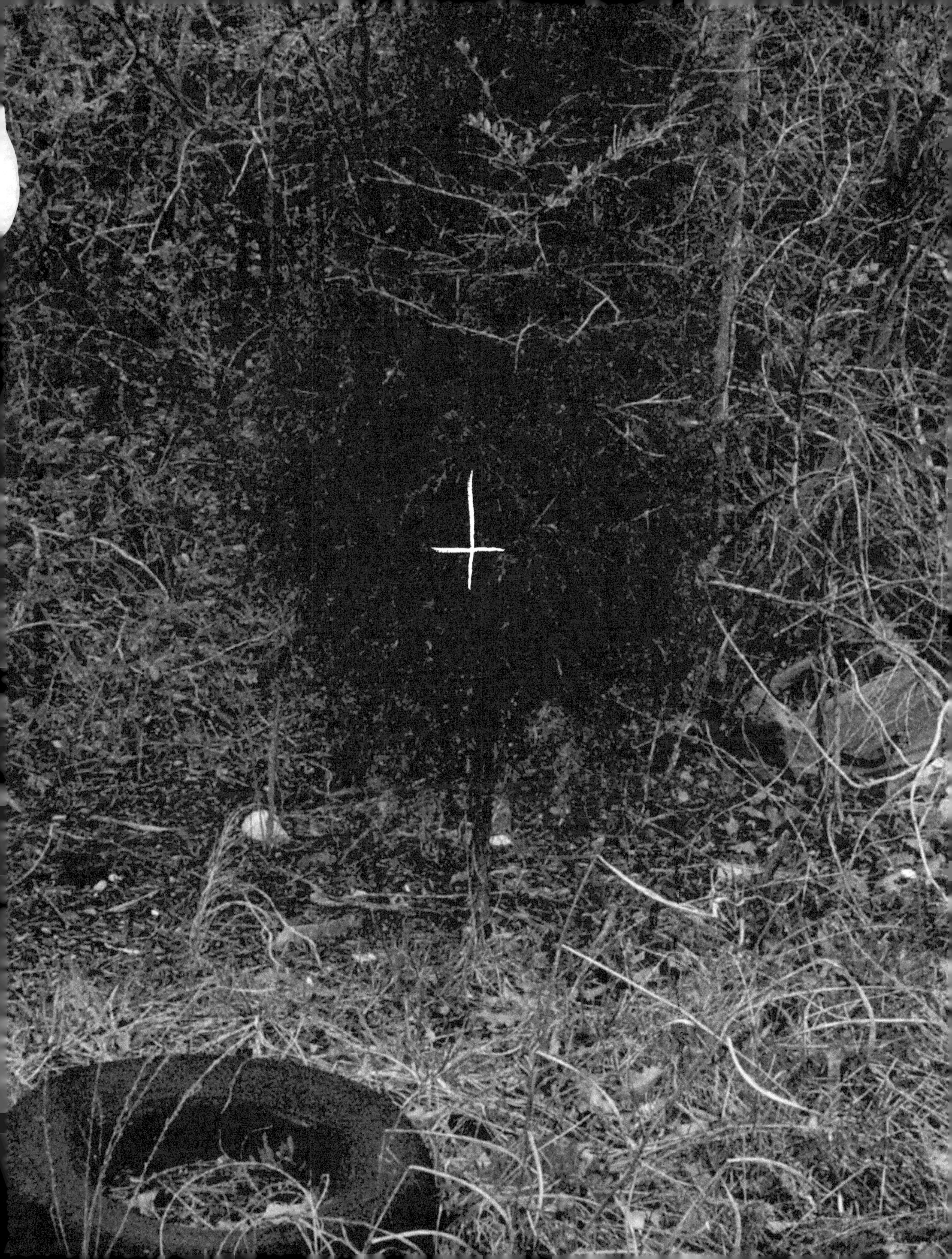

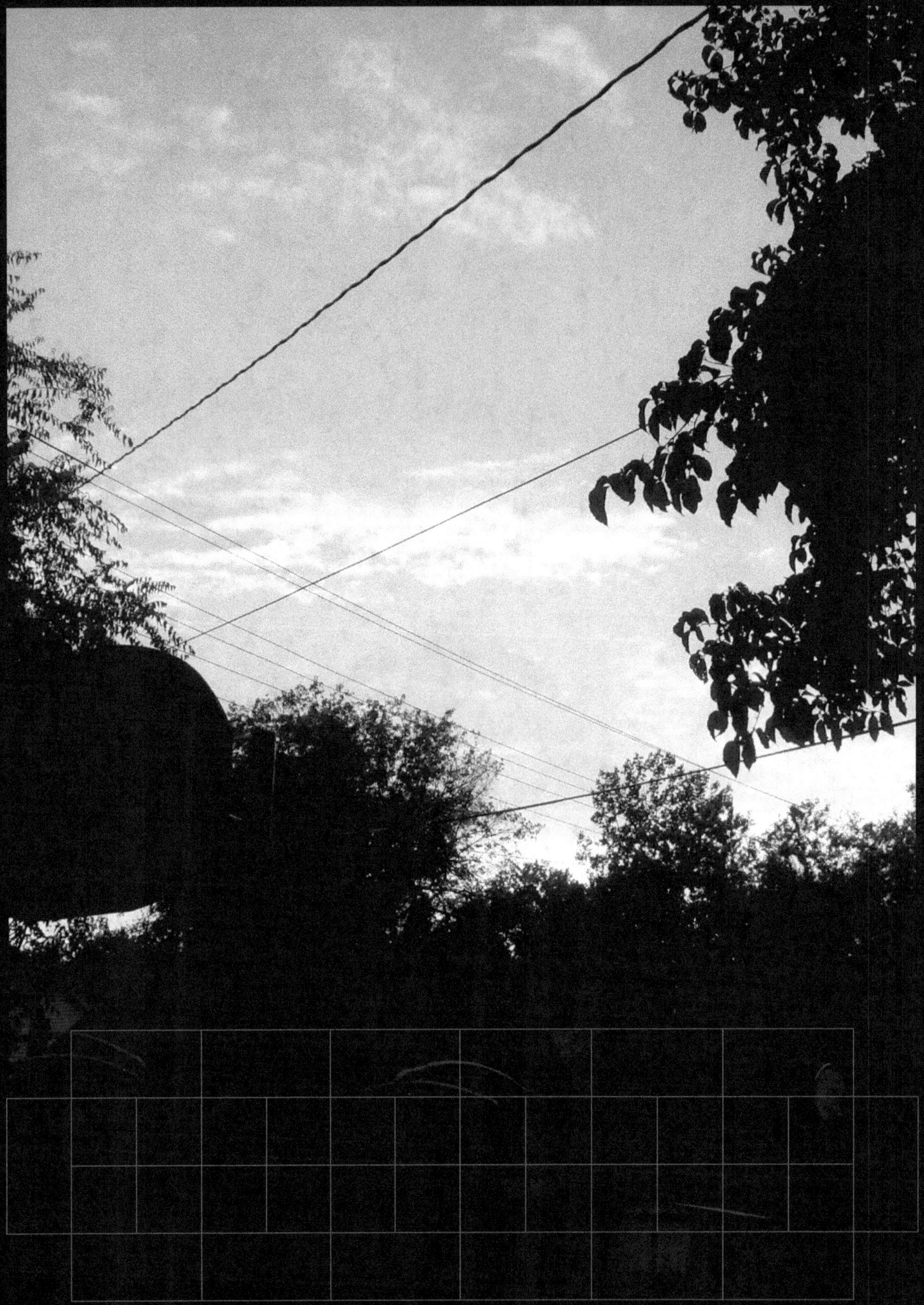

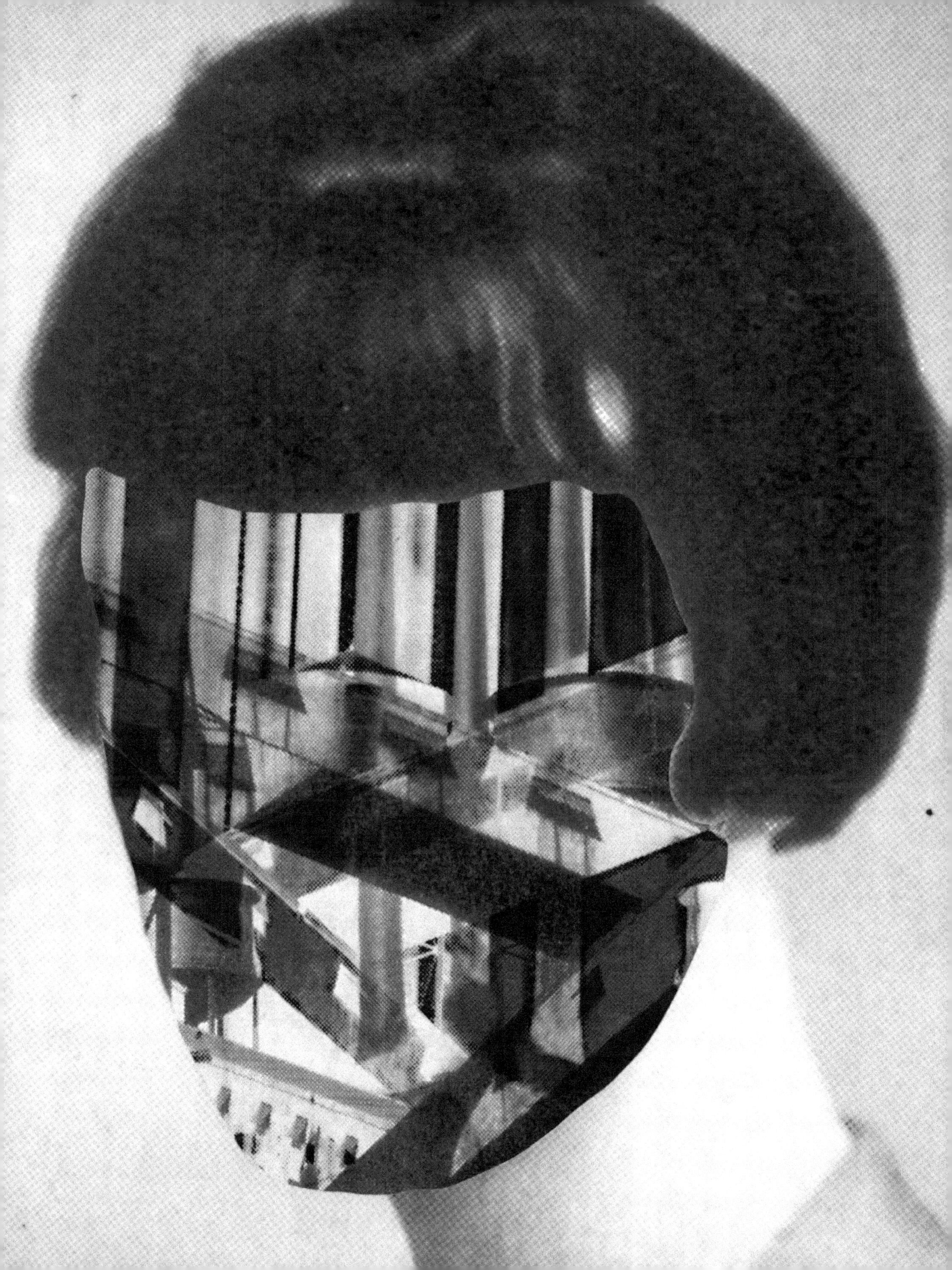

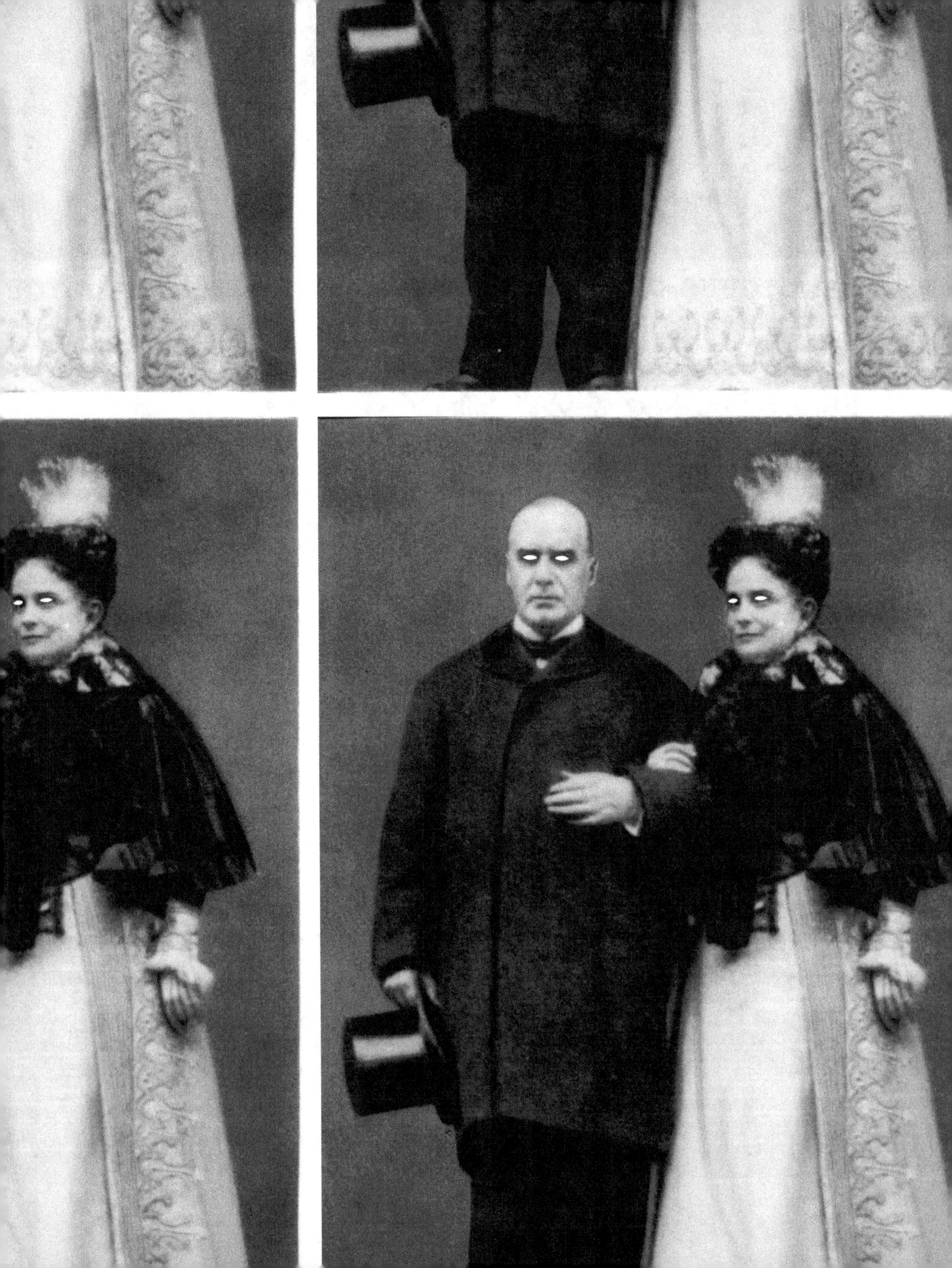

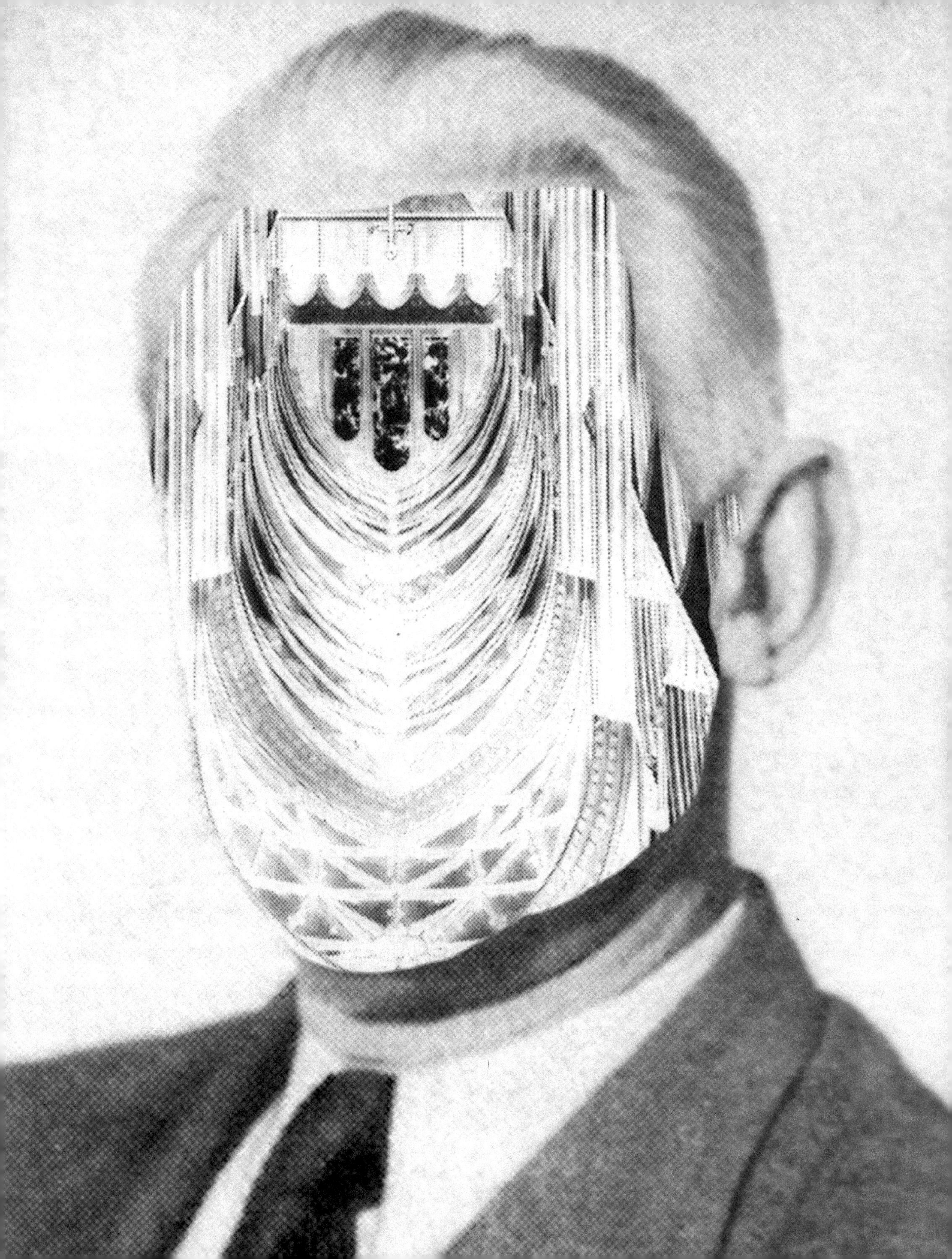

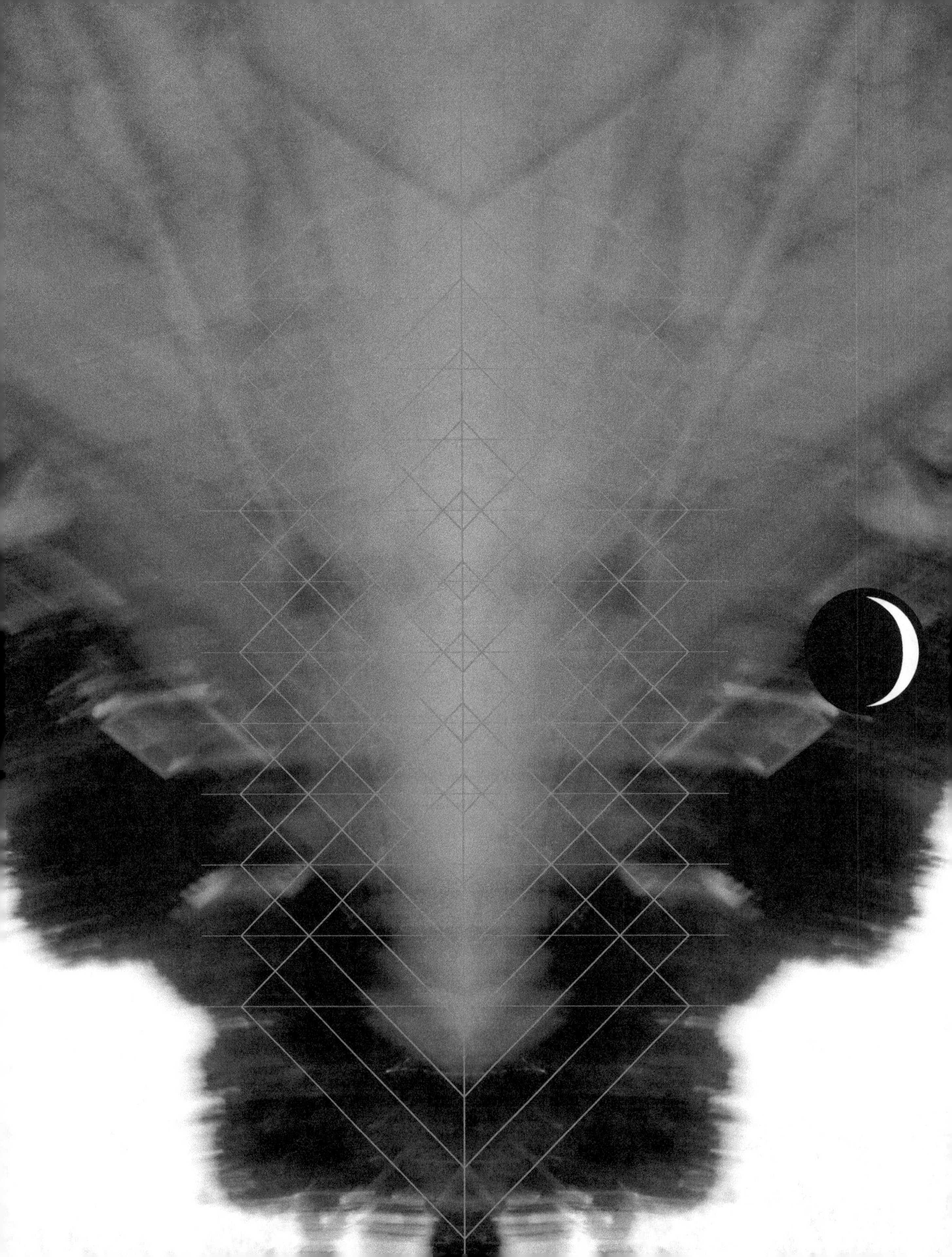

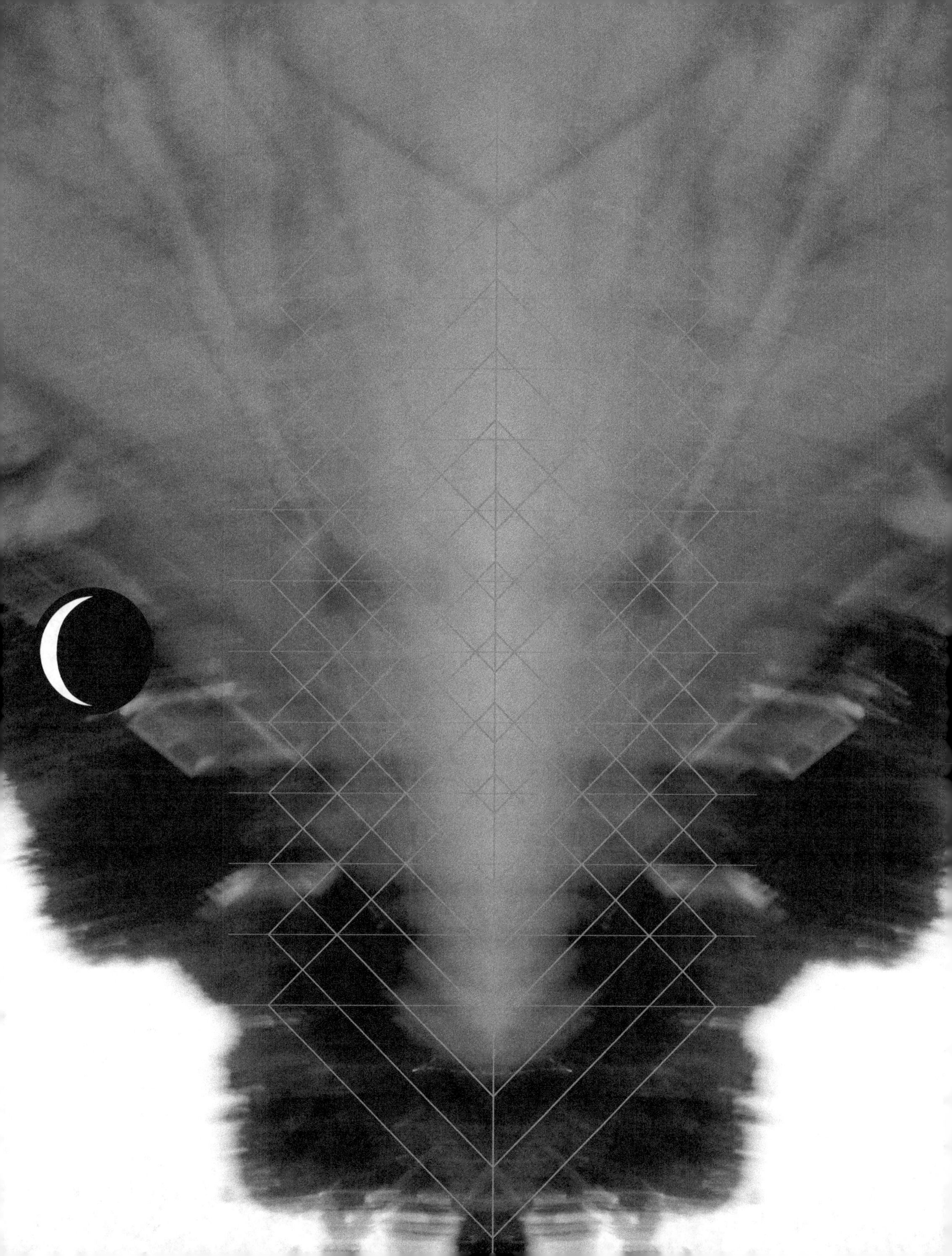

like a version, torched for the very first time.

www.ingramcontent.com/pod-product-compliance
Lightning Source LLC
Chambersburg PA
CBHW081020170526
45158CB00010B/3109